THE CLERGY DANCE

Grayson Atha

Grayson Atha is a rare human being. He is the very antithesis of the tired cliché of a preacher. Steadfastly faithful and yet irreverent in all the right ways. A compelling orator who has a great deal to say and yet seems as eager to listen as he is to speak. Grayson was the first graduate of the Methodist Theological School in Ohio, a circumstance of his name and his timing, but fitting also in the way he embodies everything we could want in a graduate of our institution.

Clergy Dance is filled with humorous anecdotes as well as profound wisdom gleaned from a very rich life. The reader will recognize a good bit of Grayson in the book and, importantly, a great deal of that deep substance of life which arises from the vocation of one who takes both God and people seriously. Grayson has had a tremendous impact on the world around him. This book offers a glimpse of the life and the world that shaped Grayson and invites the reader to engage in important reflection. It is an invitation well worth accepting and a book well worth reading.

Jay Rundell
President, Methodist Theological School in Ohio

Introduction

This is the story of the making of a pastor. It is told so my own children might remember, and our grandchildren, and also those who follow them. And I would be un-truthful if I didn't say it is also told as insurance of sorts against the possibility of fading memory in the future. In that event, I would have it as a place to which I could return, to read, to think about, and to possibly feel some of the great emotions that were woven together to create this fabric that is my life.

Also it has been written for the people of West Liberty, Ohio. It was this community that put a watermark on me early in life. Wherever I go, they are with me. Not always visible, but a part of me. I want them to know what they did. Many who had a major influence on my life are fanned out in other places—and many are no longer living. But I still want this story told to their children and grandchildren.

The storyteller will move often from present to past because, in any moment in life, we are a part of all that has been. What we remember, and even what we do not remember, all helps to shape life. And speaking of remembering, the details of some of the stories I share may have faded, but the intention—the heart—of the stories remain the same as when they unfolded.

The Theological School experience is also woven throughout this story, for theological education is not just learning about religion and the Bible; it requires one to unpack their own past—their experiences, the scars, the defining moments as well as their present faith. These are all woven together throughout the theological educational experience to help individuals enter into the ministry with a foundation strong enough to withstand the numerous tragedies they will invariably encounter and to allow them to minister to all they encounter in a way that brings people closer to God.

I would like to thank my wife, Wende, and my children, Marcus, Angelyn, and Holly. These four people, whether they ever meant to or not, have helped shape my ministry, and in this way have been partners along this journey. While I know my family feels the richness of the life we have lived, there were times they were alone and must have wondered if the journey was worth it. Consequently, there were many people in our lives who worked to make sure the five of us felt loved and supported. No matter what. My thanks also go to Cyndy Garn, a friend and colleague who helped keep the many pieces of this project together.

I would like to thank Sharon Pope for her guidance throughout the publishing process, and Jason Bradley-Krauss and MJ Vukadin at House of Krauss for working with me tirelessly on the cover design.

Reflections on The Clergy Dance

"Grayson Atha is one of the most interesting and courageous people I know. He is an advocate of human rights and dignity at all costs. This book gives us insight into his life and the events that shaped him." **Nancy M. Vaughan, MD**

What is it like to be a church minister? Let Grayson Atha be your guide in this delightful book. Frank, funny, and thoughtful throughout - like Grayson in person - the book is about faith, calling, gender, race, sexuality, the Bible, church life, family life, a cat called Maggie, and much more. **Sheena Phillips, London, England**

Contents

|

Chapter 1

"I need to talk with you as soon as possible." The urgency in her voice was unmistakable. "Like right now! May I come over to your office?"

"I'll meet you there in fifteen minutes," I said.

When I arrived at the church office, she was already there.

She wasted no time. "I've been in a relationship with someone. He kept telling me he was going to get a divorce and then we would be together. I've been waiting months for him to leave his wife. Today I was in the waiting room of the dentist's office, and his wife came in. She's pregnant."

She put her head in her hands and wept. When she looked up, her grief had turned to anger. "I hate him! I hate him so much! I want to tell him to never ever call me again."

When I was first appointed to this church I had noticed this woman. I had found her attractive and, from time to time, a fantasy would take up residence in my mind and remain until I ordered it to be gone. Now she was confiding in me about a long-time affair. I listened carefully, but that fantasy hovered around the edges of my mind. Embarrassed and frightened, I ordered the fantasy to get out. Again.

Before she left my office, I did offer to pray with her. "God, this child of yours has just been torn apart by the revelation of the last few hours. Forever you have helped put the broken pieces of life together. With your child's help, do it again. Would you bring her some peace and direction for these moments now and in the days ahead? Help her to gain perspective about what is passing and what is lasting in her life."

As she walked out of my office, I offered to meet again if she needed to talk.

She took me up on my offer. After worship the next Sunday, she asked me to stop by her home. There had been some new developments in her situation.

When I arrived at her home, she offered me a seat on the couch. We were alone. She sat down very close to me. Too close. I felt sweat forming on my forehead. I tensed up. I knew I shouldn't have accepted this invitation, but it was too late; I was already here.

I moved slightly, turned, and faced her. "So, how have the last three days been?"

She reached over and put her hand on the back of mine. "Painful, really painful. Actually, just awful."

"What has been the most difficult for you?" I asked, my heart skipping a beat.

"The betrayal," she said. "Being told he loved me and then the realization that I was crazy blind."

By this time her fingers were moving slightly on my hand. Was this involuntary or deliberate? Was she testing the waters or just hurt and disappointed and looking for reassurance?

I'll be candid. The touch of her hand on mine was quite pleasant. So, this is how ministers cross the line, I thought. It's not deliberate, not calculating, not premeditated. It happens so innocently when we are in the midst of caring and deeply relating to people. We reach into peoples' lives, helping them with disappointment, joy, defeat, illness, death, and failure. We move into the inner part of peoples' lives where emotions are rooted. This is a good thing. We *should* go there with them, for the Christ was always meeting people at their most vulnerable moments.

But we must realize this is sacred and vulnerable space for us as well.

I really did want to help her, but I knew I must separate my own feelings from the struggle of the moment. Perhaps she was interested in something more with me, or perhaps I was a warm, live, safe reality she could depend on in the midst of great turmoil. I knew this was a critical moment, and what I did or did not do would help define my ministry and the well being of this parishioner.

Does this all sound like a clinical class on clergy/parishioner interaction?

The real questions on my mind were: What do I do now? What do I say? How can I be a pastor to her yet get out of here unscathed? How did I get myself into this situation in the first place?

And why was this not covered in theological school training?

Chapter 2

In 1952, Republican Dwight Eisenhower was elected President, and there was great rejoicing on the Atha side of my family. Elizabeth Taylor, my mother, came from a long line of Democrats. We never visited my maternal grandmother in Lakeview, Ohio, without an intense discussion of politics.

My grandfather, Harry Atha, so disliked the way Roosevelt was leading our country he refused to apply for Social Security. After Roosevelt died, and Harry Truman became President, there was great expectation that a Republican would be elected in 1948.

Stanley Shenk, a well-respected pastor at South Union Mennonite Church, would come to our home to watch the election returns. Mennonites were discouraged from having televisions, but there did not seem to be any rules against watching important broadcasts at someone else's home. As far as I know, Stanley Shenk was a Republican, because he always watched the returns with other Republicans.

On election night in 1948, many Republicans went to bed believing the long absence of their party in the White House was over. Thomas Dewey had been announced as the winner of the presidential election by major news stations, but by morning, it became evident that the call was premature. Indeed, the White House would continue to be occupied by a Democrat.

However, in 1952, Eisenhower was elected while Stanley Shenk and my parents watched. They stayed up very late to be certain the morning would not bring disappointment.

The Revival Comes to Town
In this same year, Mennonites, who have a prominent place in West Liberty, orchestrated an all-out tent revival. I was born in this small town, and knew many of the people who would attend the revival.

But, more to the point, since my father was one of two attorneys in town, everyone knew me—for better or worse. Incidentally, the other attorney was Delpha Peale, our next-door neighbor and one of the first female attorneys in the area.

When the big tent started to go up, everyone in the whole town noticed. My friends and I had hoped the tent was being assembled for a circus. We fondly remembered the circus held in town three years prior. The main act was a chicken riding on a pony. Some people complained that it wasn't much of an act but, then again, some people thought West Liberty was not much of a town. So they fit together quite nicely.

My circle of friends had no complaints. No, our mistake did not lie in under-valuing the act; it lay in the fact that we thought we could copy the show. Not long after the circus was over, several of us grabbed a couple of chickens from Rufus Detweiler's Chicken Yard and tried to teach them to ride a pony at Craig's Coal Yard and Elevator. We worked nearly a full day, and even tried tying the chicken to the pony, when suddenly the pony ran away, the chicken flew, then scattered off, and we dispersed with the unspoken understanding that the main circus act was a little harder than it looked. A new respect for ponies, chickens, and those with the patience to teach one to ride the other, was born.

Seeing no animals around this particular tent, we turned to other possibilities. "What's gonna happen in that tent?" we inquired.

"A revival," we were told.

"A revival?" We didn't even try to hide our disappointment.

"Yes! There will be music and praying, and a preacher will get up and preach. Then he will ask anyone who wants to go to heaven to come to the front. Then we'll sing more, pray more, and then we'll go home and come back and do it all over again six nights in a row!"

That did not sound like much fun.

"Will this involve chickens and ponies in any way?" we asked.

The adults ignored us and continued to construct the tent.

"It is sort of like a circus," one worker said with a smirk, "but there are no animals and not as many clowns."

My friends and I knew we would show up anyway. Singing, preaching, and praying were no circus, but they sure beat watching the cars go by on Main Street, or watching haircuts at Ross MacIlvaine's Barber Shop. Not only would we be there for the first night, but likely for each of the six nights after as well. When something was going on in West Liberty, it was the *only* thing going on in West Liberty, and most everyone would be there to check it out.

The Night My Life Changed Forever

So, the second night, I was sitting close to the front when I noticed the evangelist looking my way and smiling, even nodding. He seemed to want to catch my eye. I worked hard to avoid him, staring down at my feet, looking at my friends, but within a short time I knew I was in trouble. Not only was he looking at me, he was pointing at me and insisting I join him on the platform. I stood up, unsure what to do, but there was really no choice.

Did he know I used to turn over garbage cans along the back alley of Newell Street with friends on Saturday night? I thought nobody knew about that.

And I did not have anything to do with the annual turning over of the Cook's outhouse, but did he know I was innocent?

I had been one of the ones throwing corn on Edna Frantz and Ms. Ryan's front porch when Elsie Kauffman caught us and made us pick up the corn piece by piece while Edna Frantz watched. But why would that matter now?

Maybe it was the chickens from Rufus Detwiler's chicken farm. Had they gone back and told Rufus Detwiler about how we had tried to reenact the circus performance?

We did hide cigars in the handlebars of our bicycles and sat on the banks of Mad River and smoked there, but we all thought nobody knew. Why was he calling me up there? Surely not a public confession of past sins, I hoped.

It was a long walk up to the platform. These scenarios and many others rushed through my mind. The guilt was getting the best of me.

All the music and activity had stopped, and a restless silence ensued while everyone waited for me to make up my mind. Would I join the evangelist on the platform or not? As I slowly walked up the steps, I searched the audience for my parents' faces. In a split second, I found them, only to see the same puzzled looks in their eyes they must have seen in mine. I did see my father nod just a bit and knew I had to continue my journey.

As I climbed the steps and came alongside the evangelist, he embraced me and turned me toward the audience. With all the pride in the world he said, "Sisters and Brothers! This young man before you is considering a call to enter the ministry!"

I was just as surprised by this news as the next guy.

He went on to say he'd be praying for me in the months and years to come and that all nine hundred gathered there that night should pray for me too. Then he put his hand on my head and prayed I would be further moved by the Holy Spirit to tend to God's flock for all my days. Applause erupted, and as I walked back to my seat, the choir broke out into song, "Jesus calls us o'er the tumult of our life's wild restless sea; day by day his sweet voice soundeth, saying 'Christian, follow me!'"

The tent seemed to bellow up with the cool night air, filled with the kind of possibilities and promise brought on by a sudden shift of events that occur when we are least expecting them.

How Was I Going to Get Out of This One?
Of course it was all a big mix-up. Becoming a minister was not something I had ever considered. At one point I almost confessed this

to the evangelist. He had me mixed up with someone else. This was a horrible mistake. But something stopped me. Standing in front of that huge crowd of people, surrounded by a big choir—the whole thing was kind of intoxicating. As I floated back to my seat, I suddenly realized something.

Everyone in West Liberty now thought I was going to be a preacher.

"And why not?" I asked myself.

Over the next few days, people stopped me on the street to congratulate me and report they were praying for me. I was stuck. My parents said they were pleased, although I knew my father had hoped I would become a lawyer and take over his practice.

"Why didn't you tell us before?" they asked, perhaps a little hurt.

"Well," I said, "I just sort of decided recently and didn't really have a chance to tell you."

That wasn't completely untrue. I really had decided for sure just as I was returning to my seat in that tent, with the choir's voices swelling up around me.

Still today, walking down the streets of West Liberty, where my wife Wende and I own my childhood home, people tell me they have prayed for me since that night at the revival so many years ago.

What Does it Mean to be Called?
Several times I have been a member of a district or conference committee on ordained ministry. One of the questions most often asked is, "Tell us about your call to ministry," which implies a call by God. Usually the candidate will have a story to share, and some talk about hearing God's voice or being "told" to enter the ministry. Often the experience involves their minister, a relative, or a Sunday School teacher. The stories are always compelling and moving, and they leave one with the impression that the storyteller truly has been ordained by God.

On several occasions I have tried my best to convince the committee to leave out that question. Maybe I was afraid someone would ask me about my calling, and I would have to spill out the events surrounding the evangelist mistaking me for someone else. And everyone would know my "call" was a case of mistaken identity.

Truly, once that question is asked and answered, it is difficult to say no to a candidate. I mean, who does anyone think they are to mess with an ordination by God? Who in their right mind would say, "Well, God may have called you, but we are telling you something different?"

I have never succeeded in my attempts to nix that question. One committee member gasped when I suggested it, saying, "How in the world will we know whether or not to ordain someone if we do not ask them about their call?"

My own belief has always been that there are better questions to ask. Questions about a person's life, where he or she has been and wants to go. Questions like: "How do you get along with people and why?" "What is the biggest mistake you ever made in life?" "What did you learn from the experience?" "What are your goals in life?" "What do you believe about God, and how does your belief play out in your life?"

If the candidate's answers have anything to do with helping people, you have a pretty good idea about what they believe about God and whether or not the raw material is there for the making of a pastor.

If a candidate's main goal is to make money, and they like working with people (as long as those people do their bidding), then the committee will probably be helping the church and the candidate by saying no. I, myself, have never had difficulty saying no to a candidate if I believed their life outlook would not play well in a church. It is far better for a committee to say no than to let a person continue in the process and then discover, years later, they are miserable as a minister. The church can likely survive a poor pastor, but the candidate may lose a part of his or her life that may set him or her back for years.

The Call Comes Full Circle

I would often take one of my children with me when I called on the sick and shut-ins, or attended a visitation or funeral. On several occasions, one of them would sit up most of the night with me at the bedside of a person dying. Having my children with me at hospital visits might not be on the list of "quality" things to do with your kids, but all three of them tell me today that the experiences we had together as we visited parishioners were some of the most influential in their lives. Part of the privilege of ministry is being present while life is being ushered in and out, so I tried to be present, as far as I was able, when a parishioner died or soon after a baby was born.

When Marcus, our firstborn, was nineteen, he and I were at the Madison Road Arby's in Cincinnati. He told me he was going to be a minister. I was surprised and pleased, but I attempted to restrain my joy. And, of all things in my response, I said, "Tell me about your call from God."

"Well," he replied, "I have watched what you do, and I think the ministry is how I want to spend my life. Not only that, but I think I can do a really good job."

I do not want to dwell too long on my own viewpoint of a call to ministry, for I am aware that my thinking is in the minority of those who try to sort out persons who should and should not be passed along the lines of candidacy. However, the track record of our present system seems to have some wide gaps. Note that fifty percent of those who say they are called to ministry drop out along the way either before ordination or after serving for a time in the local church. What happens?

Some readers may feel I am simply trying to cover up the evangelist's "mistake" so many years ago or perhaps rationalizing my failure to speak up and say, "Hey, you have the wrong person." And, of course, I would not discount completely the possibilities that the Mennonite evangelist had a strong grasp of being God's agent to become the caller of young people. About that time, four other persons in West Liberty chose the ministry. If indeed that was a method he used, he would be close to the Christ Jesus method of saying, "Follow me."

11

Never once do we read of Christ talking to a follower who heeds the call and saying, "Now tell me about your call." Christ's word was "Follow me, and later you will begin to put it all together."

Some in the church like to say to persons considering the ministry, "Don't choose to be a preacher unless you come to the conclusion you can do no other. Resist the call until it is so vivid you must say yes. The road is hard, and you will become discouraged. The ministry will call you to sacrifice money, family, and your future."

Granted, there are trying times in the ministry, but that is also true in all professions. Besides, United Methodist pastors have guaranteed appointments, a place to live, a pension among the most secure in the world, and medical insurance. But all of that does not begin to touch the great meaning that comes from being one who provides leadership for a church.

A Life of Meaning

A colleague, Chuck Loveless, once told me about an attorney whose father was a pastor and related to him this story, "I have had a good life as an attorney but nothing like the meaning my father had. When he retired and walked up the aisle his last Sunday, people in the pews reached out to touch him as he walked by. And why not? He had married their children, buried their parents and loved ones, was there when the babies were born, showed up at the hospital bed when sickness would not let go of its grasp. My father's life was woven into the very fabric of the people of the church, and one has to search far and wide to find a life occupation that will provide the meaning that comes along with the ministry."

In writing these thoughts and reflecting on my own call to ministry (or lack thereof), I do not mean to doubt or belittle anyone else's call. At the same time, I am inclined to believe we may have placed a bit too much dependence on a divine call as the primary ingredient to making a minister.

My concern is this: when we attribute this to ministry only, then what of the lawyers who really care about their clients and teachers whose lives become intertwined with their students? What about physicians who, like my own physician, Dr. Bope, spoke at a funeral for a family of a patient who had never connected with a church? Are there not many physicians who would make excellent pastors, and are there not many traits of a physician that are minister-like? And what of the pastors who lack the caring traits of human understanding and kindness? And what about the evangelist who calls on the wrong person to join him on stage?

Or was it the right person after all?

What about when a 19-year-old says, "I watched what you do, and I not only think I can do it, I want to do it"?

Is there a possibility we just might be able to include in a call the demonstration of traits and characteristics that are Christ-like, and with theological training and further church experience, the pastor *and the calling* will come forth?

Perhaps we should look for these traits in children and youth, and then call them ourselves, telling them that later they will be able to put it all together.

Grayson Atha

Chapter 3

When I was nine, my parents became greatly interested in the church. Being present at the local Methodist Church was important. I vividly remember the pastor's prayers were long, and his visits to my grandmother, who lived three months each year in our home, were regular and extensive. Although I never stayed around for the whole visit, we would be called together for the prayer marking his departure.

Then we had a change of pastors. The new pastor's prayers were short, and his sermons were fascinating and seemed to end soon after they began. I was intrigued by his style and his communication of the Gospel, but something happened, and my parents stopped going to the Methodist Church.

In Search of the Perfect Church
We began attending a church called Wesley Chapel five miles out in the country. When my parents became displeased with this church and quit going, it was college time for me, and so I left the local church scene in West Liberty.

Years later, when my parents had both died, I asked my brother why they had left those churches. He was not certain, although he thought it might have been because the pastor had a mustache or wasn't biblical or they did not feel "fed."

I remember one time the minister spoke disparagingly about Billy Graham and, when my father confronted him about it, the pastor did not back down. I think that is when my parents left the church. Although they attended various churches from time to time, and they financially supported the church, they really never got involved again. Neither did my brother, nor one of my two sisters.

I believe the early years in a person's life are a great influence on the rest of his or her life. The community I was born into had tradition and long-held understandings. There were about thirteen hundred people in West Liberty and a lot of churches—three Mennonite Churches, a United Methodist Church (Methodist while I was growing up), a Congregational Christian Church, a Church of God, a Presbyterian church, Grace Chapel (non-denominational), and a couple other independent churches.

People would grow unhappy at one church and go to another. Sometimes the unhappiness was so intense they would go to a church in another town or start another church. But West Liberty was a religious community. All stores were closed on Sundays, and when I was growing up, seldom would there be any manual work done on Sundays. If someone was in need, everyone pitched in to help.

My Business is Your Business
For the most part, everyone knew everyone else, and there was an unspoken awareness of what went on in the community. When both of my parents died, and it was my task to clean out their house, I had placed about forty garbage bags on the curb. Six months later, someone asked me if I meant to throw away the family pictures. The person asking me the question did not have them but knew someone who thought they knew someone who had the pictures. No, I did not intend to throw them away. A week later, the trash bag of pictures was sitting on the front porch.

We had crank telephones and operators. One time several of us were making prank phone calls to Fannie Trummel. Fannie was one of West Liberty's most colorful characters. The operator said to me, "I'll put this call through, but if you make any more calls, I am going to tell your parents."

Once when I was traveling home with a female friend, and an ice storm stranded us, I called to tell my parents I would not make it home. After the phone rang several times, the operator said, "Grayson, I do not think your parents are home. Hold on, I will check around." Soon she came back on the line and said, "They are at your Uncle Kent's. They are coming to the phone now."

16

Soon after Wende and I were married, we were visiting my parents, and Wende mentioned she would like a kitten. My father rang up the operator and asked, "Ida, do you know where we could get a kitten?" A few moments later, Ida called back with three possible sources.

Maybe sometimes the operators knew more than they should have, but their knowledge of the community often rescued a life, discovered an elderly person in trouble, or stopped a child from making prank calls. In West Liberty, we had call waiting and call forwarding long before it was discovered and sold as an additional service.

Grayson Atha

Chapter 4

In his book, *Imprints: The Lifelong Effects of the Birth Experience*, written in 1984, Arthur Janov makes this case: events that happen at birth influence our life. Even though we do not remember the events, nevertheless, they help shape our actions and thinking.

There is a story in the Bible about Elizabeth and Mary, both pregnant. Mary was carrying Jesus, and Elizabeth was the future mother of John the Baptist. When they met, the baby leapt in Elizabeth's womb indicating some kind of awareness of Jesus' presence.

There were two events that happened in West Liberty long before my birth that I believe had an impact on my life and specifically my ministry.

A Tale of Two Stories
The first event was important because it was forever talked about.

In 1870, an extensive fire destroyed much of the business district of the community. At that time, my grandfather was three years old. He often told how his father, Simeon, awakened him and took him to see the fire. On numerous occasions, he related this story.

The second event was not talked of at all.

Around 1866, a member of the Piatt family came home after fighting in the Civil War and brought a person of color to West Liberty. There were few people of color in West Liberty at that time, but this man, Edward Jackson, had served with Mr. Piatt, and he came to West Liberty with great recommendations. Mr. Jackson was a freed slave. He started a livery stable in West Liberty and became quite successful.

He and his wife had a son, Grant. Grant Jackson was handsome and well-liked. He worked at the Depot[1] meeting trains and helping with luggage. Many of the arriving passengers would ask for Grant, much to the disappointment of other baggage handlers. Some time later, Grant got in trouble and was put in the West Liberty jail. The jailer left the door to his cell unlocked, and a group called The Regulators broke into the jail, tarred and feathered Grant, and sent him out of town and told him never to return.

But he did return, and Dr. Ben Leonard, a West Liberty doctor, tended his wounds. Some time later, a resident of the community hit Grant in the head with a rock and crushed his skull, causing his death. The alleged murderer was convicted and placed in the Ohio State Penitentiary but was released after a few days. Later some of the people of the community rose up and broke windows out of the Jacksons' house and ran the family out of West Liberty.

I had to work hard to find the details of this story, as it was taboo to talk about the Jackson family while I was growing up.

On the other hand, the story of the fire was repeated often in the community, and today there is even a community-wide yard sale called The Annual Fire Sale. As I mentioned, my grandfather repeated the fire tale often, although he was only three when it happened. He was 15 when the Jackson family was run out of town, and he never talked about that story. In fact, no one mentioned it. Though many knew something big had happened, silence reigned.

Then, several years ago, a retired airline worker, Lane Bliss, moved back to West Liberty. As a child, he had heard his grandmother talk about the story but, when he would ask about it, his grandmother would hush up. So he determined to do research, and when he called me to his home later, he had newspaper stories from as far away as California telling the story of Grant Jackson. It was not a pretty picture, and I could well understand why the community acted like it never happened.

---

[1] The Depot is located on North Detroit Street and is now known as Marie's Candies.

When Grant Jackson was murdered, the local Methodist preacher held the service in the Jackson home on Main Street. The home was filled with people, and those who could not get in stood in circles around the home several persons deep. Perhaps remorse was settling in.

Lasting Imprints of the Past

Later, I will write about my appointment to an all-Black Church. I felt completely at home from the moment I walked into the church. Why? I do not fully know, but somehow I wonder if the events before my birth, and a community called to pray for me (who could pray but not talk about their sins of rejection and racism) played an important role in my comfort level.

My roots run deep in West Liberty. When my parents died, we bought the house on Baird Street where I grew up. They moved there when I was two, and it is now a place where we gather with our children and grandchildren for rest and rejuvenation. It was in this town that the evangelist prayed the prayer that helped determine my future. Seated in the tent that night were those who knew the Grant Jackson story well, but it was buried deep within them. All my life people have stopped me on the streets of this village, and even in the halls of Green Hills Care Center, to remind me that they remember me and have prayed for me.

In the hymn, *Rescue the Perishing*, the third verse reads in part, "Down in the human heart, feelings lie buried..." Those who study the ways of human behavior say those buried feelings, from time to time when we least expect, rise and influence our thoughts and decisions. So sometimes I wonder how the imprint of Grant Jackson on the community of West Liberty may have imprinted and affected my ministry at times.

Fairview Cemetery is located on a hill overlooking West Liberty. A town meeting was once called to decide if Fairview should be considered a part of West Liberty, or should the West Liberty signs remain at the beginning of the cemetery but not include the cemetery?

The usual questions were asked: what about liability; would we tax those buried there; would West Liberty be responsible for snow removal; and would those buried there count as part of the West Liberty census?

Jake King stood, and in a voice easily heard by all, said, "Count? Do we count them as a part of the community? Why most of us think often about someone buried up there. They influence our lives, our decisions. They count! They always have, and they always will. Makes no difference where we decide to put the Village sign. Those up there always have and always will be a part of this community."

When Jake sat down, everyone seemed ready to go home. No vote needed to take place. Everyone agreed with Jake and quietly everyone left the gathering place at the Town Hall. The next day, Bruce Johnson[2] pulled up the West Liberty Village signs, carried them through the gravestones, over the hundreds who were buried there and firmly planted those signs just past the last grave. To this day, Fairview is still within the Village.

Grant Jackson is buried at Fairview but in a section without markers. The exact location of his burial is unknown. I believe it is overlooking the Village. My grandfather's father, Simeon Atha, who took my grandfather to see the fire in 1870 is buried there along with my parents, grandparents, and the evangelist who prayed for me. They all rest in the great sepulcher of the earth, together with secrets hidden deep within the human heart.

---

[2] Bruce Johnson could neither hear, nor speak. He was known by the whole community. He was a self-appointed police person in West Liberty. He was often seen directing traffic whether needed or not. He regularly attended the Methodist Church.

Chapter 5

When one ends up in a particular profession, she doesn't get there alone. Every minister, teacher, lawyer, physician, father, grandmother—everyone—is shaped, in part, by those who nurtured them early in life. Wherever we go, whatever we do, we are accompanied by a multitude of those who have lived and contributed to our lives, in big ways and small. We cannot discount those who no longer live and walk this earth. Indeed, they are much a part of our call as well.

I have officiated hundreds of weddings. Every time there is a wedding, a whole host of people shows up, above and beyond those visibly seated. When two people join their lives as one, anyone who has ever touched their lives is present in spirit. This is true in much of life. We are surrounded by a host of those who no longer walk the earth but who are ever present. The Bible calls them "a great cloud of witnesses."

Right and Wrong

I didn't choose my college; my parents did. Taylor University, a conservative Bible-centered institution, was founded in 1846. My years at Taylor were an affirmation of the conservative theology of West Liberty, my hometown. The school leans toward a literal interpretation of the Bible. They have sent out a multitude of graduates in all walks of life—teachers, scientists, business people, coaches, and clergy—with deep faith commitments.

Whenever I visit Taylor for an alumni gathering, at some point, someone representing Taylor will say, "Taylor has not and will not change from the beliefs that have made her a great institution."

There is a tendency among theologically-conservative churches and institutions to be on guard against opposing beliefs and assure others that a change in basic beliefs has not and will not happen. According to them, there is a right way and a wrong way to understand God.

Choose the right way, and you will end up in eternal bliss. Choose the wrong way, and you will be cast out.

At Taylor, we were exposed from time to time to other religions but, even then, there was clarity about the right way to believe. At one chapel service, a rabbi was invited to speak. Nine hundred students packed into their assigned seats in the chapel and sang the designated opening hymn: *Stand Up, Stand Up for Jesus.*

In those four years, while working with other students and outstanding professors, my mental capacities began to stretch and grow. There are bits and pieces that will be with me always, like this word from Dean Milo Redigar (he later became President): "Whenever you act in life, ask yourself: if everyone did as I am doing, what would the world be like?" That statement often caused me to pause in the midst of making a decision.

The Sting of Rejection
While in college, I read the five books required to become a local pastor in the church. I then appeared before the District Committee on Ordained Ministry, and a few months later, the Conference Committee in Lakeside, Ohio. They judged me "not ready for ministry" and turned me down.

Maybe I should have told the evangelist at the Mennonite Tent Revival he had the wrong person.

When the Committee turned me down, they said I could try again but I should get to a Methodist Theological School. About this time, as I was feeling some rejection from the church, a well-known United Methodist lay evangelist, Harry Denman, was invited to Taylor for a preaching mission. He was known for his forceful and powerful preaching style, and although it has been over fifty years since I heard him, I still remember some of the texts he used and the stories he told.

Students were invited to make appointments with visiting speakers, so I made an appointment with Mr. Denman and shared with him what was on my mind:

"Why," I asked him, "would I want to be a Methodist preacher and have some bishop tell me where I am going to serve, and what church and house I will live in? Why can't I just pray and ask for God's guidance and have God direct me?"

Mr. Denman thoughtfully replied, "Wherever the Bishop sends you, there will be people who need to hear of the love of God. What makes a difference if it's a group the Bishop chooses or a group you believe God helped you choose? Besides, being appointed by a Bishop who also prays about his [there were no female bishops back then] decision is a whole lot better than having a group vote on you every Thursday night after prayer meeting."

He had a good point.

So, graduating from Taylor, I promptly went to Goshen College Biblical Seminary, a Mennonite school. The Methodists were building a Theological School in Delaware, Ohio, but it was not yet accepting students.

I spent two years at Goshen and, during that time, I enrolled in a course in preaching. The time arrived for me to preach before Paul Miller, the homiletics professor, and the class. When I finished my sermon, Professor Miller put down his pen, paused for a long time, and said, "Mr. Atha, you just broke many of the rules of preaching."

My heart sank.

He wasn't finished. "I am really at a loss as to what to say to you except... *don't change a thing*."

His encouraging remarks were just what I needed to restore confidence in myself and my call.

Seeing God in a New Way
It was Paul Miller who gave the first lecture I ever heard about female images of God. Around this same time, the Methodists ordained the first woman pastor, but there wasn't much talk about feminine images

of God. And there was Paul Miller at the Mennonite seminary, with his black suit and clerical collar, looking to give the Methodists a few words about women. He had a captive audience in his students, and his words were powerful.

"When Junior has a father who is an alcoholic," Professor Miller explained, "and that father comes home at night and Junior hides under the bed in fear, do *not* talk to Junior about God as a loving father. Junior will best learn about God if you talk about God as a loving mother, because his mother is the one who feeds, clothes, cares for, and protects him from harm."

Later I was to discover that the Mennonites, with their scholarly conservatism, were leading the parade of ways to understand and communicate the love of God, unconcerned about whether God was portrayed as male or female.

How Should We Read the Bible?
One of the first courses I took at this Mennonite seminary was *The Gospel of Luke* taught by Howard Charles. I had entered that seminary believing that if Taylor had a conservative approach to scripture, then this Mennonite seminary would take it a step further in the conservative interpretation of the Bible. Little did I realize that a process was unfolding in my life where I was beginning to rethink theological concepts I had been taught growing up in West Liberty.

When I was a young boy, Martha Hartzler and Nellie Warye, two wonderful, loving, nurturing women, had a children's time every Wednesday evening at The Congregational Christian Church. Flannel board stories and singing with great enthusiasm was the order of the day.

We had several songs we sang like there was no tomorrow: The B.I.B.L.E. Yes that's the Book for Me and We Are Going to Heaven on the Bible Club Express, The Letters on the Engine Spells J-E-S-U-S, the Engineer calls 'All for Heaven!' we gladly answer Yes. At that moment, Nellie Warye would pull out her handkerchief and wave it in the air, and all of us would follow. We are going to the mansion on the Bible Club Express!

When Martha Hartzler told us the story of Jonah and the whale and, with sparkling eyes, would say "I believe the whale swallowed Jonah, don't you?" we would answer, "Yes! I believe the whale swallowed Jonah, because the Bible says so, and if the Bible said Jonah swallowed the whale, I would believe that also!"

Each Wednesday evening, all who wanted to accept Jesus were to stay after the dismissal. I, myself, stayed several times.

In the church where we met for Bible Club, the beloved pastor of many years, Reverend Wearly, attended a general meeting of the denomination. He was not a dynamic preacher, but he was a kind, caring pastor and had won the hearts of most people in West Liberty. When he retired, the whole community held a gathering at the old high school. Leo Aschraft, a prominent town leader, presented Rev. Wearly with a brand new Ford. I was particularly struck, because they had somehow put the car on the stage in the high school auditorium.

One thing that further endeared him to the community was that he and his wife had several sons who were tall and really good basketball players. Because of these boys, several basketball championships came to the West Liberty community. One of his daughters married a terrific coach, Pearl Bechtel, who coached West Liberty to the championship. Of course, Rev. Wearly would have been beloved without the basketball championship, but this enhanced his image.

When Rev. Wearly returned from the National Conference, he brought stories of how some long-held beliefs might be open to careful examination. For instance, would salvation in Christ be possible if Mary was not a virgin? And, if we get stuck on the whale swallowing Jonah, then might we be missing the point of the story of why Jonah resisted going to Ninevah? Is every word in the Bible to be taken literally, or are there deeper meanings the writer, inspired by God, is attempting to convey?

As you might imagine, people really got stirred up in West Liberty.

Rev. Wearly was a gentle man and, although he would not hold to the beliefs he heard at the national church gathering, he was not one to pound the pulpit and declare war on those who proposed such ideas. However, it should be noted he was the one who brought home the ideas and made them known in the community. But there were many who loudly and explicitly proclaimed, "If every word in the Bible cannot be taken literally, then how can any word be trusted?"

As you know, this argument continues to divide Christians across America to this day.

So, a group of people decided to start a new church where only the traditional beliefs and understandings long held would be the rule of the day. In their view, giant theological questions had already been answered. To raise questions and doubts was to attack the faith long held. There were many theologians in the community, and they began to take sides, often without thinking carefully through the issues.

A family in the community invited the new gathering of people to meet in their recreation room in the basement. Many people from the Congregational Church and other churches joined them. By this time, I was at Taylor, but my heart was with those who had started a new church. I assumed the Taylor faculty would be in favor of the new congregation. Isn't it interesting, that when we hold a belief that, to us, is truth, we naturally assume others think like we do?

This is not always the case.

Years later, I realized there were professors at Taylor who encouraged all of us to use our minds. They felt beliefs were open to discussion, that theological inquiry was okay, and no one need leave his mind at the door that opens to faith. For many of the big questions of life and belief, the evidence is not "all in" after all.

In fact, faith itself means the evidence is indeed beyond a final intellectual cataloging.

Chapter 6

Dr. Charles, of Goshen Mennonite Bible Seminary, opened his class on The Gospel of Luke by telling a story taken from an issue of *The Reader's Digest*.

A young person approached a college professor and said, "I have decided to become a medical doctor. Will you help me?"

"Of course," the professor replied. "Go into the next room, take the jar off the shelf, and look at the preserved fish inside. Write down what you observe."

In a few minutes, the young person was back with the list. "Very well," said the professor. "If you still want to be a doctor, come back tomorrow."

The next day, the young person returned, and the professor gave the same instructions. The aspiring doctor replied, "I did that yesterday."

"Indeed, you did," said the professor, "but, if you want to be a doctor, you need to look further."

The young person looked again and did find some things that had escaped observation the day before. For five days, the same instructions were given. Just before the young person gave up, discouraged, the professor said, "Now, take the fish out of the jar. Touch it. Now that you are able to get closer, what do you see?"

Finally, the professor said to the young person, "To be a physician you must be willing to work hard at finding the answers. A quick glance, or even one session, will not provide you with enough evidence for reaching a decision. To be a good physician, you cannot just rely on what others tell you without looking for yourself."

Then Dr. Charles said to the class, "We are about to examine the fish called The Gospel of Luke. The first week we will consider the first four verses."

How will he spend a week of classes on four verses? I thought.

In Which I Break Into a Sweat
Dr. Charles continued, "First we will look at each word. Beginning to my left, we will go around the table and consider each word and its part of speech."

My neck tightened. I began to sweat.The parts of speech and I? We had never really gotten along. I could read. I could write. But matching individual words to their parts of speech? Forget it. What would I say when he got around to me?

I listened carefully as each person got it right. I looked at the words, guessing which word I would get. I looked for clues in other words. I searched for any little bit of help. Then I counted my classmates and the number of words in the text. I was seated two persons away from Dr. Charles, on his right. The class was big. I glanced at my watch. With the introduction and the fish story and my place in the room, the clock might just become my friend. Several times, there was discussion about a particular word. This was good. However, my turn was fast approaching.

Suddenly, I remembered a story my brother once told me. He was teaching a group of scouts and had to write on a chalkboard. For a moment he panicked, thinking he might misspell a word. (Neither of us were excellent spellers.) So, as he wrote, he told the scouts, "Some words I will spell right and some words I will spell wrong. See if you can tell which is which."

"If you are not smart," he told me, "you need to be clever."

Ten minutes to go, and Dr. Charles was moving in on me. Three students away. I prayed. I raised my hand.
"Yes, Mr. Atha?"

30

"Why is it important to identify each part of speech?" I asked. "Why are we doing all of this?"

"An excellent question, Mr. Atha."

I had hit the jackpot. No, I was not just being clever—even Dr. Charles said it was a good question. But, wait, maybe not.

"Mr. Atha, right now we are examining the fish, and we will not really know all about the fish unless we are willing to look carefully at each part. Each part is crucial to our understanding of the whole."

"Each part," he repeated for emphasis. He began a discourse on how each part is crucial. I thought I was in the clear until the person one over from me got up and left the room. Now, that is clever! I was now third in line. I had uncertainty about that part of speech. But the words flowed out of Dr. Charles' mouth about how, if one ignores any of the parts, then one is not able to accurately comment on the whole.

The bell rang. My prayer was answered, and I was not about to analyze the theological meaning of the words "my prayer was answered." We had gone through 47 words. There were 77 in all. If I sat in the same seat next session, and Dr. Charles started at the same side, we would run out of words before Dr. Charles ran out of students.

At the start of the next class, I took the same seat. He again started on his left.

Studying God's Word: A Life's Work
Something had happened in that class as we worked our way through Luke under the guidance of Dr. Howard Charles. The Bible is a wonderful book filled with magnificent lessons and deep truth if one is willing to come back to its message day after day with an open heart and mind. This truth became crystal clear when I stopped by Dr. Charles' office to ask a question about the class schedule. I was going to miss the class that day, and I wanted to report before class began.

When Dr. Charles opened his door, it was evident that he was hard at work.

"What are you working on?" I asked.

"I'm preparing to teach the class you are going to miss."

"I thought you said you have taught this class for twenty years!"

"Yes, that's true," he said, "but, if I do not spend at least four hours preparing for each class, I feel I go unprepared. After twenty years of teaching this class, I am amazed at how much I learn each year."

I had no words.

"Mr. Atha," he said, "I have discovered that we can spend our whole lives studying the Bible and, when we finally sleep with our ancestors at death, we shall not have grasped it all. But, in God's wisdom. the whole of God's love is open to everyone. Even those who might not know each part of speech."

Chapter 7

I left Goshen College Bible Seminary realizing I was on a journey—a journey that started at the beginning of time when the Creator called us into existence. A journey I could not—and would not—take lightly. A journey I wouldn't take alone.

A journey I would invite others to go on with me.

The lessons I had learned from Martha Hartzler and Nellie Warye, and all the pastors of the past, were moments of introduction to the great teaching of the Bible. It would take more than a lifetime to grasp its depth.

Although theological education is an important element in making a minister, it is only part of the equation. Experience in the local church makes theological education come alive.

Diving in to Ministry
I was assigned to a four-point circuit of rural churches while I was still a student at The Mennonite Seminary. Wende and I were married on Valentine's Day, 1959, and lived in Goshen, Indiana until October of that year when we moved into the parsonage in Haviland, Ohio. We were enthusiastic to receive this appointment, and the church provided a great foundation for a continued education of college and seminary. There were four services on Sunday morning– 9:00, 10:00, 11:00, and 11:30 am. Training in the local church began immediately.

At the time we were introduced to the Charge Committee, the chair announced that new cabinets were to be installed in the parsonage kitchen before we arrived. A member of the committee from the smallest of the four churches said, "I thought we were not going to put in the new cabinets unless the new pastor absolutely demanded it."

Before I could say, "We can get along with what is here," the chairperson, Virginia Gudakunst, hit my arm with her elbow and said, "No, we are going to put in new cupboards. They will be installed right away."

"Well, how much will they cost us?" asked a member from the smallest church.

"The cost total will be $1,600. So 15% of that would be $240," responded the chairperson.

"Well, I'll have to see if the church will go along with that," she said.

The chair responded, "I am absolutely certain that, when you tell the church about the new parsonage family, they will be happy to help all of us get a good start. Especially with your powers of persuasion."

It was a small exchange in the committee, but it was a valuable lesson the classroom on Luke could not convey. In the local church, lessons are taught that have no other source.

No Beating Around the Bush

Three months later, after the last service of the day when I greeted people as they left the church, I discovered the willingness of some people to say exactly what is on their minds.

One older gentleman passed me and said, "Reverend, if I am sick and in the hospital, don't come calling on me. And, if I die, don't bother coming to the funeral home. If you can't come to see me when I am well, don't bother to come when I am sick or dead." And he moved on.

People gathered around me and apologized for him. "Don't let it get to you, Reverend. That's just the way he is."

But I did think about his comments much during that week. Do I just pass it off and, if not, what should I do or say?

The next Sunday he was in church and, when he passed me, I said, "I have been thinking about what you said last week. I have been here three months and I have not been to your home. I was wondering if you might give me another chance? Could I stop by your home next Tuesday afternoon about 2:00 pm?"

"Yes," he replied quickly, "and I'll tell you a lot more that's the matter with you."

On Tuesday, I arrived at his home with a yellow legal tablet and pen, ready to write down the wisdom he possessed.

"Look," he said, "your calling is one. Three months and you did not call in my home. The second thing, I am not sure you are well-versed enough in the Bible to be a preacher. And the third thing is, how old are you anyway?"

"Twenty-four," I replied.

"Well, you are too young. Our Savior was 30 when he started. Maybe you should have waited."

That's all he had. Just three things, and one he had already shared. That day I decided he just wanted to be heard, to be taken seriously. I was a bit surprised at how short was the list of my faults. Where was this long list now that I was in his home?

Actually, he had provided a great gift to me early in ministry. I learned that, when someone lets you have it, take that opportunity to help him go deeper into what is really happening, and often the harshness disappears. The next Sunday, he gave me two jars of green beans and tomatoes from his winter storage supply.

Life and Death
The first call for a funeral came after I had been at the church for two months. A family had an aunt in Fort Wayne who died at 100 years of age, and a pastor was needed for the funeral.

I had no idea how to do a funeral.

I called and asked the Methodist pastor in the next town for advice. "Oh, it's easy," he said. "Doing a funeral is quite simple. You will do well."

"How long have you done funerals?" I asked.

"About 20 years."

"Well this is my first, and it does not feel simple," I told him. "May I come over to your place, and will you walk me through it?"

"Sure," he said, "but didn't they teach you how to do funerals in seminary?"

I mentioned something about the parts of speech and then said, "I do not remember."

The visit was helpful and reassuring. And so was the call to Mike Williams, an old college friend with a good sense of humor.

"I have a funeral tomorrow for a woman 100 years old," I told Mike. "Quick, tell me what to do."

"Read the 100th Psalm," he said.

"What does it say?"

"I don't know, but most of the Psalms are pretty good. And there are 150 of them, so unless you get someone older than 150, you will always have something."

When I arrived at the funeral home, the funeral director had placed the speaker stand facing the deceased. If she opened her eyes, she'd be looking right at me.

"Could the casket be closed before the service begins?" I asked the director. I needed to give myself the best chance possible to get through this first funeral. It seemed easier if the dear aunt was not looking my way.

"I will check with the family," he replied and quickly returned to tell me, "No, they want her to be able to hear the service. When the music stops, you begin. Turn off the light on the speaker stand when you are finished. That way we will know when you are done. When you switch off the light, it turns off a light in the office, and we will be right in."

The music stopped, and my first funeral was about to begin.

"Make a joyful noise to the Lord all the earth;
Worship the Lord with gladness. Know that the Lord is God.
It is God who made us and we belong to God.
We are God's people and the sheep of God's pasture.
Enter God's gates with thanksgiving and God's courts with praise.
For God is good and His faithfulness is to all generations."

Mike was only joking, but he was right; that 100th Psalm worked. I glanced a couple of times at the deceased; her eyes were still closed. I remember the time Jesus raised the dead, and thought, "Please, Jesus, not now."

"The God who created us and lovingly placed us in this world—the God who sustains us throughout life—is the same God who meets us when we die. We should have no fear."

No fear, I told the friends and family gathered. I, myself, was shaking, but I got through it. The first funeral was history, and I had survived.

Life: the Greatest Teacher
"Don't they teach you that in seminary?"

As a matter of fact, they do not. Theological school is not a *how-to* experience. Theological school does not have mock weddings or funerals, no practice baptisms, not even a practice session of someone unloading their frustrations on you on the way out of a church service. Seminary may touch on these, but they are not the main things.

37

What theological school does is to help students grasp the unfolding drama of human history, the acts of God through human history, the understanding of God throughout the ages, and those who almost get it right and those who almost totally misunderstand.

Theological school does not teach a student how to conduct a child's funeral, but it does, through an unfolding drama of human history, prevent a pastor from standing at a child's graveside and saying to the parents, "God took the child because God needed another angel." Theological school equips a pastor, so they do not say to a family who loses a member to cancer, "Well, this was God's will."

Chapter 8

Bernice Slane was dying from cancer. She was thirty-five and had four children, ages thirteen, nine, seven, and four. On a Friday evening, I stood at her bedside as she breathed her last breath. Bernice and her husband were a part of the Haviland congregation.

That very day, in another of the four churches, a tragedy had been averted. Ken Williamson, from the Latty Church, had purchased a new tractor. He was crossing the railroad tracks when the tractor stalled. The sun was setting in the west and prevented him from seeing a train bearing down on him. Ken heard the train whistle and jumped from the tractor.

When Life Doesn't Make Sense
The struggle over simple answers to the complex situations of life played out early in my time on that four-point charge.

The next day, at the Haviland Church, there was great sadness and despair over the death of such a young mother. At Latty, there was much rejoicing over the narrow escape of Ken Williamson. He told the congregation that, when he jumped, as he hit the ground, the train sliced the tractor in two. People were praising God for deliverance.

"God was with you, Ken," they said. And, of course, I joined in the rejoicing.

But I struggled. If God was with Ken, then what of Bernice Slane? Was God not with her? How does one become God's agent of rejoicing with a near tragedy averted and, at the same time, an agent of comfort when death to cancer could not be avoided?

This is the kind of life situation theological school helps students wrestle through. Of what value is it to know how to go through the motions of a funeral if one has not grappled with the issues of life and death? And, when the seminary has helped students struggle with these issues, the student does not just go through the motions; he or she walks through the valley of the shadow of death with the family.

Why Do I Believe What I Believe?

After my third year on the four-point circuit, The Methodist Theological School in Delaware, Ohio was receiving students, and I transferred from the Mennonite Seminary. In the meantime, I had taken a couple of summer courses at Garrett Theological School in Evanston, Illinois.

There, a professor of an Old Testament course infuriated me with his method of teaching. Actually, he was helping me wrestle with some of the great mysteries of the Bible, but he just did not fit into my earlier Bible Club teaching prototype from the basement of the Congregational Church. I resented him because I believed his teaching was inconsistent with those early flannel board stories (if it's in the Bible, I believe it).

Every year in West Liberty, after Bible Club ended, we would do a 15-minute program over WIZE in Springfield. When I learned five Bible verses, I had the privilege of speaking into the radio microphone. Of course, the speech was prepared and given to me, but to a nine-year-old, speaking to thousands (Hundreds? Dozens?) of listeners, it was a wow moment. I stood proudly in front of that microphone, with WIZE emblazoned across the top, and gave my speech. "God said it. Jesus did it. I believe it. That settles it."

But Charles Kraft, this Old Testament professor at Garrett, was raising some unsettling questions. I had taken my early concepts with me to seminary, and I was looking to have them reinforced, but the Mennonites, Garrett, and soon the Methodist Theological School, would ask me to engage my brain. I was being encouraged (forced) to think realistically about what God had said and what Jesus had done. I had to ask myself: had I developed my own beliefs, or was I simply accepting the beliefs handed to me?

This was not a comfortable inquiry to make.

I slowly began to discover that those early-instilled beliefs were firmly imbedded. Although I was open to new Truth, the Bible Club teaching still hung around. I held on to the old, even as the new—fascinating, believable, and reasonable—began to take up residence in my brain. Both lines of thought were fighting for real estate in my mind.

And the battle wasn't pretty.

The undercurrent, in both West Liberty and at Taylor, was that one had to be careful about seminary. "Just when you are least expecting it," they warned, "your faith could be challenged and sometimes even taken or 'stolen' from you!" In the seminary setting, you must protect your beliefs beyond anything else, or you could be robbed in broad daylight in one little Bible class."

I kept feeling there must be a better way, a way to build on the old as we learned new things.

Isn't that what higher education is for?

Growing Into My Faith
Theological school forces a student to keep reciting the long-held truths but also to unpack and analyze them, struggle with them, and then embrace them into one's own life. In theological school, no one gives you a speech and tells you to repeat it. Seminary takes you through the struggle of human history and God's revelation so the speech becomes your own as it is woven into the fabric of your life.

When one goes to medical school, each student is assigned a cadaver. As part of their medical education, the students dissect that cadaver piece by piece. Part by part, they examine and seek to understand the make-up of the human body. And, when knowledge is gained about this one body, the student has basic knowledge of all human bodies, as they are basically the same.

But, for the theological student, there is no cadaver. The human being provided for the theological student is his own being. The main purpose of theological training is to enable the student to delve into

41

her own life, her own existence, and then to begin to understand herself alongside the great span of human history. Each student begins to grasp the way God has acted to call the creation to newness and wholeness.

If this does not unfold for a student in seminary, then theological education has not happened.

When a person graduates from theological school, and the transformation has not taken place, the new preacher will soon be discouraged. He will search for meaning in all the wrong places—in a materialistic way of life, in a society driven by money. He or she will have some ability to articulate religious concepts but not enough. This can only lead to despair, discouragement, and resentment.

One of the most valuable experiences for me in theological education was hearing of others' experiences in the local church. Each week our professors would share real-life examples with us, and we would discuss and process these ideas and issues in the coffee shop and dining room with other students serving a variety of churches. This interaction was very helpful to me.

Chapter 9

At my first appointment, the four churches were located close together. Scott and Haviland were two miles apart; Latty was located five miles north; and Broughton was two miles to the east. In the center of the four churches was The Consolidated School. Naturally, I wondered if these four churches could consolidate and perhaps even build one central church across from the school.

I was already well aware that presenting major decisions took time, so I asked for a Study Committee composed of three people from each church.

Change: A Tough Pill to Swallow
In the meantime, I sought out Dr. Browning, a Christian Education professor and a process genius at the seminary.

"Trying to bring four churches together is a huge task," he said. "Many pastors have been brushed aside and burned in the emotions that surface during the process of change, no matter how needed that change might be. Let me offer you an idea you can keep in your pocket. You may find it helpful now and throughout your ministry."

"People resist change. Knowing that, you offer an alternative to radical change and provide a way for the congregation to experience change without the permanence."

"I suggest a twist on the old parent/child negotiation routine. You know the one. The parents say to the child, 'Just try the vegetables. One little taste.' Eventually, many children begin to like food they were not even willing to try at first."

"Parents are very wise when it comes to helping children accept what is good for them. If they said, 'Now, eat this vegetable and, for the rest of your life, you will make it a regular part of your diet,' parents would have a real battle on their hands. So will you, unless you find a way for the four churches to experience being together and see how much they like it after all."

One block from the parsonage sat the old Haviland School. It had been closed since the Consolidated School had opened. I hoped the four churches might be willing to have several days of evening meetings there, like the Mennonite Tent Revival in West Liberty. Bonus: we wouldn't even need a tent. The old Haviland School auditorium would be the perfect place. Many people from the four churches had, at one time, attended this now-closed school.

The idea was presented to the four churches, and there was no opposition. It seemed everyone was willing to taste the vegetables. The Haviland Church had agreed to provide their piano, and Scott church would move their electric organ to the Haviland School Auditorium for the meetings.

But not too fast. Clarence Adams had a problem.

"Who said you could move our organ?" Clarence said, following a worship service.

"At the last meeting," I said, "the Church Board said Scott Church would be willing to move the organ for the week."

"Well, *The Book of Discipline* says the Trustees make decisions about church property," Clarence argued, "not the Church Board."

"Well, you have a good point," I said, "but I was thinking since all the Trustees are on the Church Board, and the decision was unanimous, the Trustees were okay with it."

"Not all the Trustees were at the Board meeting," Mr. Adams said, "and, further, it was the Board, not a meeting of the Trustees. Besides, I am a Trustee, and I was not there. Now, either you call a meeting of the Trustees, or don't move that organ one inch."

The Trustees met ten days later on a Wednesday evening. After a brief discussion, a motion was made to move the organ to the school for the week of meetings. The motion had a quick second.

"The organ was purchased for the church," Mr. Adams said, "and it cannot be moved to the school unless all those who contributed to the purchase of the organ agree."

When the vote was taken, it was seven to one to move the organ to the school for one week.

Three guesses as to which member cast the dissenting vote.

"Let me say one thing," Mr. Adams stated, as the meeting was adjourned. "If you dare try to move that organ out of this church, I will park my truck across the entrance and throw away the keys."

What was a pastor to do?

Giving People a Voice
Back at the seminary, I stopped at Dr. Browning's office to tell him of the vegetable tasting at the four churches and the standoff over the organ.

He invited me to sit down.

"This is not the last time you will experience this," he said, "if you choose to stay in the local church. This very situation is the reason some pastors decide to leave.

"You need to hang in with this man. We live in a world where choices are limited. This man must buy a license each year for his truck. He receives a property tax bill, and he has to pay it. The same for state income tax and federal taxes. The state tells him how fast he can drive. Sometimes church is the only place where a person can be boss.

"You are on a good track to help the church experience life together," he said. You have a chance to make it with this gentleman. You can overpower him and leave him bleeding along the wayside, or you can attempt to find out what is going on with him. I suggest making a call in his home and initiating a conversation about the situation. You may be surprised to learn his story has nothing to do with the organ."

That Sunday's text was the story of the Good Samaritan. "Jesus told a story of a man traveling along a road, when robbers ran out of hiding, beat him up, took his money, and left him there to suffer. Three different people came along and observed his situation. Two ignored him but the third, a foreigner, helped him up, put him in a motel, and paid the bill to give him a chance to recover."

As I preached the sermon at Scott, I kept hearing Dr. Browning's words, "You can overpower him or try to understand."

That afternoon I stopped by Mr. Adams' home. He was reserved but invited me in.

"It is obvious you care deeply about the church," I said, "and I want to try to understand what you are feeling about the organ. I have watched you, Mr. Adams. You do a lot to help other people. I believe you have a good heart, and I wanted to talk with you to see if there were issues I have overlooked. I believe these meetings at the old school would be a good thing for the whole community. Would you be willing to tell me what you are thinking?"

He was willing. "I think you are just like my two sons when they want something," he said. "They just keep at it until I give in. Sometimes it feels like I don't even count. I'm just here to do what they want."

The conversation went on for an hour. We talked of his experiences at the Haviland School and how he got involved in the Scott Church. We talked about his involvement in the community, how his parents taught him to help others, and how much he enjoyed it.

A month later, the day before the gathering was to begin at the Haviland School, Clarence Adams did park his truck at the entrance to the church. He also helped load the organ on the back of his truck and onto a large styrofoam pad he felt would be helpful in protecting

46

it. I watched as he carefully covered the organ with blankets and drove it over to the Haviland School.

People like Bob Browning have taught in Theological School for extended periods of time. The disciples they've made with their teachings of Christ may well live on in many churches and lives for years to come.

Grayson Atha

Chapter 10

Front row seats at concerts, plays, and sporting events are the most desirable (and expensive), but those same seats in classrooms and churches often sit empty. However, in my New Testament class of 45 students at the Methodist Theological School in Ohio, I always sat on the front row.

I think, as I reflect back, I chose the front row seat because, somewhere inside of me, a voice was saying, "Get ready. God draws nigh. The hour has come and now is."

How We Read the Bible
One particular lesson stands out in my memory. The text was John 11, the raising of Lazarus. What better moment in which to bring all my West Liberty knowledge and seminary training? Was there any Bible story more poignant than this one about a miracle of bringing the dead to life?

Dr. Gealy began the class by reading the story from his Greek New Testament. He didn't read in Greek; he translated the Greek into English in a smooth stream. He read at a slow pace, pausing from place to place to emphasize a word or a moment in the story.

"When she told Jesus of Lazarus' illness," Dr. Gealy read, "Jesus stayed two days longer before he responded to the request to come to his friend Lazarus' home."

At this, Dr. Gealy paused, rattled the change in his pocket, paced, and implored, "What kind of person waits two days to go to the bedside of a sick and dying friend? When we read the stories of the Bible, we read them through our own eyes and interpret them with our own powers of reasoning. As students of the Bible, you will use the Word to speak and teach about God's love. You will call people to follow Jesus. So, if you look at this story in a literal way only, then you will likely instruct people to wait a couple days before they respond to friends' pleas to visit their death bed."

My World Turned Upside-Down

Literally was the key word here. The words spoken by Martha Hartzler in the basement of the Christian Church knocked on the door of my mind just then. If the Bible says the whale swallowed Jonah, then I believe that. There was the literal interpretation of the Bible, and yet, Dr. Gealy had stood in front of us and gave a twist to the literal word. There was an adjective he threw in there. If we look at Jesus' delay in a literal-only sense, does literal mean Jesus waiting two days? The Bible says, "Jesus waited two days." God said it; Jesus did it; I believe it; that settles it. But, here on this front row of the New Testament Class, Dr. Gealy had asked if the one we will call people to follow did indeed wait two days to go to the bedside of a dying friend.

"Dr. Gealy," I said, "the Bible says Jesus waited two days. Now, if he *didn't* wait two days, exactly how long did he wait?"

"Well, Mr. Atha," he said, "how long would *you* wait?"

"I would have gone immediately," I said, "if a friend was dying or in trouble."

"Does it disappoint you that Jesus waited two days if you would have gone immediately?"

"I guess so," I said, "but it also makes me wonder why Jesus waited."

"Good, good," Dr. Gealy said. "Class, listen up. Mr. Atha has just given us a clue to understanding the message of the Bible."

Now he really had me. The Bible has clues?

"You see, class, if you are going to fully open the truth of God to those you are called to serve, you must be willing to look for clues in your study of the Bible. Mr. Atha is correct. He would not wait two days, and neither would any of the rest of us, so the reader must ask herself, is Jesus dealing with something more here than a sick friend? Then your task becomes to investigate and discover why the writer of this story said, 'Jesus waited two days.' When something does not fit, it is usually a clue to go deeper."

The class ended. "We will resume the story tomorrow," Dr. Gealy said.

I walked out of the room with my good friend and fellow seminarian, John Petrie. "John!" I exclaimed. "I have no idea what that man is saying. I just don't understand!"

And John, who was raised a Nazarene and attended a Nazarene College, replied, "Maybe you do not understand because you don't want to understand. My guess is you really *do* understand."

I did understand John's reply, and I was starting to get where all this was going. A little bit anyway. But what about all my summers at Bible camp at Winona Lake in Indiana? What about those wonderful years in West Liberty with the flannel board stories? All these things were deeply implanted in my mind and emotions. Something inside was pulling at my being, but the things I was learning in my New Testament Class didn't feel consistent or cohesive with those teachings from my childhood.

Besides, I had never made peace with Charles Kraft at Garrett. I was still angry with him, and I was not about to let go of that.

Not Going Down Without a Fight
I went to the next class prepared and raised my hand as soon as Dr. Gealy finished his opening prayer, which was almost always the same.

"O God," he would pray, "raise us from the dead that we might have new life. Open our eyes that we might be able to see, to *really* see. Amen."

"So, Dr. Gealy," I asked right away, "if we raise the question about Jesus' two day delay, are you saying Jesus did *not* delay two days?

And, before you get to it, are you also going to say that Jesus did not really raise Lazarus from the dead?"

I was on to him now. "If so, I'm not really sure where to go from here. Should I just throw away all my past and what I have been taught about the Bible?"

"No one should ever think about discarding the past," said this very wise man. "Your past is essential to understanding the present and moving into the future. Further, I am not telling you what to believe or what not to believe. This class is to assist you in understanding the New Testament so you can help others live abundant lives through the Bible."

He continued. "When you come to a story like this, you must at least ask the questions, "Is this story only about the raising of the physical dead? Or is there any death in every society, in all generations, that binds and destroys people, deaths that in some ways are even worse than physical death at times? You are going to be pastors. All of you must decide for yourselves if you are going to be pastors who raise the physical dead, or will you seek to raise to new life the lost, the discouraged, and the downtrodden? Will you go to your congregation after one has died from cancer and say, 'It is okay! I will raise them back up in a day or two!' If Lazarus were simply raised from physical death, then at some point wouldn't he need to die all over again?"

"There are many walking through life with their heads down, seldom thinking about God, never knowing God breathed into them the spirit of life. They often plod through life believing they are completely on their own. It's everyone for himself. When they pray, they pray that old prayer, 'Bless me and the wife and our two children; us four and no more.' They fail to see the connection they have with the whole human race. If they ever pray the Lord's Prayer, when they say 'Our Father,' it never occurs to them that all the people of the world are their brothers and sisters. They are the walking dead, wrapped in the grave cloths of ignorance, looking away from God, believing they are all alone.'

"My friends, they *can* be called from the dead; they *can* live again. And it is not just others, *it is all of us* who over and over need to be called from the dead because we forget, and life is quick to bind us up, and sometimes it gets so bad that, like Lazarus, we begin to smell. But God stands in the *presence* of death and calls us forth to life."

With New Eyes

And just like that, my secure, all-knowing world, rooted in the sureness and safeness of West Liberty, Ohio, was tipped on its side. The contents spilled out, calling to be re-examined, scrutinized, and turned over and over as I tried to make sense of the truths Dr. Gealy had just spoken against the teachings of my childhood.

All the while reminding myself, "You don't have to throw any of it away."

I left the class wondering if Dr. Gealy's remarks were what some people would refer to as "faith destroying." But, somehow, my faith didn't feel weakened. I was afraid, in many ways, but I also knew deep within my heart that my faith had just been strengthened in ways I had never expected.

Chapter 11

The appointive system in The United Methodist Church is a gift. Pastors do not choose where they will go, and congregations do not choose whom they will get as a pastor. A Bishop, aware of all the churches and pastors, makes the decisions. After six years, I was moved from these four churches to a church in Toledo, Ohio, as a minister with youth.

Monroe Street Church was a big congregation. All four churches of The Haviland Charge could have fit into the church sanctuary at Monroe Street. The number of junior and senior high youth was greater than the number of members of the four churches combined.

In many ways, I was not prepared to meet the church needs of all of these young people. Although I was barely thirty, the atmosphere in Toledo was far from West Liberty or Haviland. However, there was a good staff headed up by Dr. Paul Vandegriff as the senior minister. He was an outgoing, optimistic man in his mid-forties.

Standing Up for What's Right
At the seminary, I had been taught relationships were primary in the work of a pastor. You must identify with the person or family with whom you relate. You dare not simply be a detached observer. You must remain in control of your own life while being willing to try to understand the dynamics of a person's situation. You must also be willing to speak truth to those who take advantage of others, who make decisions without an attempt to understand the dynamics of the people affected.

Sometimes, to do that, you will need to take a stand. That stand might be uncomfortable at best and most likely frightening and disruptive to your life.

Two of the professors at seminary had taken a stand and landed in jail for it. The Dean, Van Bogard Dunn, and the Old Testament Professor, Dr. Everett Tilson, decided to attend a Methodist Church on Easter Sunday morning. So far, so good. But, it was the late 1950's, and they went to church with people of color. The two professors were white.

In those days, churches of the South (and many of the North) were not open to people of color.

Their group, which included two Bishops of color, was denied entrance to the sanctuary. When they protested, they were arrested and jailed. When the church realized they had turned away Methodist pastors and bishops, the church paused briefly to reflect, but the event caused many Methodists to realize there was a major injustice going on here. Not only was it un-American, it was far from anything Jesus ever taught.

These two men were reminders daily on the seminary campus that following Christ often came with a price. Their very presence there among students in theological school was a powerful reminder of the possible outcome of ministry in the Methodist Church.

When at the Haviland charge, I had been asked to help plan and lead a large number of district youth in an all-day gathering. We chose the topic of Segregation and the Bible. It happened to be the title of a book written by Everett Tilson, one of the professors at the seminary.

Once the Youth Conference was advertised, there were angry letters written by some individuals that this was no topic for youth to consider. I began to experience the uneasiness that comes in the life of a pastor. The mayor of Van Wert was to give a welcome to the gathering of youth, but his office called the day before and said the mayor needed to be out of town and could not welcome us. It was the first of many times I would feel the conflict of knowing I was doing the right thing, while realizing I was leaving angry people in my wake.

Over the years, I learned to cope more effectively with that, but one never really sheds the weight that comes with knowing you are angering some, as you create change for good in the world for others.

It is especially difficult when those you anger are people you respect and care about very much.

Now, in Toledo, open housing was making an impact on the community. Al Reed, who was African-American and a Methodist pastor, was also a student at Methesco. Al was forthright and insisted his church take a stand on the issue of open housing. I had a great respect for Al, and I spent much time thinking about what I should do.

I, myself, could not really grasp that a person in this country who had the money was prohibited from living where they chose. I had seen the movie, *A Raisin in the Sun*, and knew that was the case in Chicago, but surely not in *my* city.

I See It with My Own Eyes
Then I ran into Roma and Ed Blunt, an African-American couple who were lost one day in Toledo and asked me for directions. I suggested they allow me to lead them to their destination. They agreed and, from that point on, a friendship developed that would change my life.

Several weeks later, I contacted the Blunts and invited them to dinner. During our time together, I asked them if all this talk of open housing was true or if people were being denied because they lacked resources. They explained that they were actually in the process of looking for a house or apartment to rent, and Ed invited me to his office the next day to listen to some telephone inquiries he planned to make.

When I got there, Ed had a *Toledo Blade* newspaper open to the For Rent advertisements. He began to go down the list of homes and apartments available. He had a speakerphone, so I could clearly hear the exchanges. Most went something like this.

Ed: Hello, I am calling about the house advertised. Is it still available?

Renter: Yes, it is.

Ed: Does the advertisement reflect everything about the house, or are there further things you would like to share?

At this point, their words would be affirming and positive with the hope of closing a deal soon.

Ed: When would it be possible for my wife and I to come look at the house?

(The time would be arranged.)

Ed: I suppose this does not matter to you, but my wife and I are Black.

(usually a pause)

Renter: Well, you are right, it would not matter to me, but it would to the neighbors and I really do not think you would be happy in this house.

Ed: Well, how about you meet us at the time you suggested, we'll see the house, and then go from there?

A variation of this would come out:

Renter: Well, there were some other people who looked at the house and were going to call me back this afternoon. If they do not want the house, and it is available, I'll call you back.

After about ten calls, I left Ed's office that day very troubled and absolutely convinced that white people were being treated one way and people of color another. The issue of money, credit worthiness, down payment, and first month's rent did not matter.

People were being told "no" for one reason—because they were Black.

A march to support open housing was scheduled for the following week. The march would go through a neighborhood where the battle lines against renting or selling to Blacks had a stronghold. When I walked out of Ed Blunt's office, I knew I must march in that parade.

The next day I called Dr. Tilson at the seminary and told him about the march. "I am an associate pastor with two hundred teenagers," I said. "How do I approach my senior pastor about participating in the march?"

Dr. Tilson replied, "You go to him and tell him you want him to know from you that you are going to participate in the march. You do not need his permission. This is your decision, but you must be aware there may be consequences."

My Pastor Surprises Me

The next day I went to Dr. Vandegriff's office and said what Dr. Tilson had suggested. He leaned back in his chair. "Do you have a plan for when angry parents call you about your participation?"

"I'll try to explain what the problems are for black people related to housing and help them understand why I felt it was important to march," I replied.

He leaned across the desk. "Good luck, because when people are filled with emotion, they don't hear explanations. What if the Staff Parish Relations Committee takes you to task? Are you okay with that?"

"I think I am," I replied, feeling that familiar weight return.

"How are you going to get to the march?" he asked.

"I guess I will drive over. A church has offered its parking lot."

"Would you like to ride over with me?" he asked.

"*You* are going to the march?" I asked.

"Why, of course!" he responded emphatically, and I realized I wasn't the only one with equality on my agenda.

Although I was determined to march, knowing he was marching too was a pleasant relief and a good example for a senior pastor.

The Sunday morning of the march, Dr. Vandegriff preached an unforgettable sermon titled, "No More." I still swell with pride when I think about the courage it must have taken for him to preach this sermon. He told of the Coliseums where, centuries ago, Christians were thrown to the lions.

Then he said, "No more, that day is long gone."

We heard about the auction block where slaves were sold, the factories where children worked, the voting booth that barred women.

"No more, that day is long gone."

He ended his powerful sermon by saying, "In the name of the Creator, and being led by the Creator, we will look back someday and say there was a day when people of color were confined to certain parts of the city, they were not free to live in other places, *but no more*. The day is far past when, in this great land, we can say no to any citizens because we do not like the color of their skin."

"Reverend Atha and I will be participating in the march this afternoon. If you want to join us, meet at the church's front entrance after worship."

Standing for Justice
Many people chose to go out the back entrance that day, but many also gathered at the front entrance, including about fifteen teenagers, and together we marched.

As I marched, I experienced, for the first time, the power of large groups lining the streets shouting names, holding up signs that degraded people. There were threats made, and I must admit I felt fear. So this is what it means to take a stand! To stand against the angry shouting people who lined the streets.

The tasks of ministry were taking on new meaning and leading me toward a future of standing where the Creator called.

Chapter 12

As we got close to Christmas, Jim Martin, another associate pastor at the church and a long-time friend who had also participated in the march, asked me what I thought about Roma Blunt being Mary in the Christmas pageant. The Christmas pageant had been a forever tradition at the church. Over one hundred children annually participated.

"Think you can pull it off?" I asked.

"It's worth a try," he said, not missing a beat.

On Christmas Eve, when Mary and Joseph walked down the long aisle of the sanctuary, Mary was Roma Blunt, and she was carrying a Black Baby Jesus.

I looked over at Jim Martin. He winked.

It was a wonderful Christmas pageant.

Divine Appointments?
The United Methodist appointive system enabled me to have the growing experience of 200 youth and a brush with open hostility while taking a stand. As I reflect on many years of ministry, which included seven different appointments, it is tempting to believe that a group of people working with the Bishop had assigned me to places that would develop my character and understanding of ministry.

Frankly speaking, the appointive system of the Methodist Church is generated by need. Church leadership speaks often of long-term appointments and getting the right person into the right place, but the reality is that most appointments happen because a pastor is needed in each church. Often the good intentions and goals fall by the wayside.

As I was leaving Toledo for Norwood, Ohio, one of the youth came into my office with a tip about my personality that has proven very helpful over the years. Nancy Griener sat on the floor beside my desk chair and said she thought she should go to Norwood with me.

"Why?" I asked.

"Well, when you came here, I did not like you," she said, "but after a while I really got to liking you. I think you affect many people that way, so I would like to go and tell your new congregation that, at first, you will not like him, but wait a little while and then you will."

Of course, it did not work out for Nancy to go along to the next assignment, but I took her story and told it at each new church. It proved to be a wonderful way to get started.

Chapter 13

The assignment was Norwood, Ohio surrounded by the city of Cincinnati. When we first received the call, it was to a church in Dayton. Wende and I drove there, walked around the neighborhood, looked in the windows, and began to adjust to the change.

Three weeks later we were assigned to Norwood.

"What happened to Dayton?" I asked the Superintendent.

"Well, someone at the Norwood church knew the candidate from another church and had a negative experience with him, so they were reluctant to accept the appointment. We decided to send him to Dayton and you to Norwood."

We Are All God's Children
Prayer and God's leading are wonderful concepts, whatever they mean, but I have just described the appointive system in reality. It may or may not be God's way, but it most surely fits Harry Denman's criteria of an appointment: make sure there are people who need to know the love of God, and seek God's guidance to help you make the best of it.

Norwood was a community of 30,000 (mostly white) people, and it was perceived that there were structures in place preventing African-Americans from moving into the community. I once asked Sam Wright, a Black pastor friend living in Cincinnati, if he thought Norwood had structures to keep Blacks out.

"No, I do not think so," he said, "but you see, Grayson, when Black people move, they want to move up, and Norwood does not afford that opportunity."

Touché!

Norwood was a good community, and Grace Church was a wonderful place to fellowship and raise children.

I was asked to be a part of a community committee called The Norwood Improvement Committee. This is where my children were being educated, where Wende and I worked, and where most of my parishioners lived, so I was ready to help. On the Committee were business, financial, public service people, and one clergy.

In the midst of our meetings, but separately from the Committee, I wrote an open letter to the Mayor of Norwood, Don Prues. In the letter sent out to the entire congregation, I asked if Norwood would not be a better place if we welcomed all, if all of us could experience the wide variety of people in the world. In the next meeting of the Improvement Association, I was taken to task by the chairperson for sending the letter (and mentioned the Association in the letter). I was not asked to resign, but it was clear that the mayor might be making that decision.

In the next few days, the Mayor called and invited me to lunch. I thought wouldn't it be simpler just to tell me on the phone rather than a painful lunch to administer the coup d'état. However, to my pleasant surprise, he thanked me for the letter and stated that some of the things about the community had clashed with his Catholic teachings. He believed it was positive that a religious leader had written openly about some of the structures of the community that had remained unspoken.

My Family Pays the Price

The open letter now had wide circulation, and I began receiving letters of opposition and support. I printed each letter in the church newsletter with a response. Over 90 letters were received, and I interspersed the negative with the positive.

This time became a great learning experience for our children and me. Our youngest child, Holly, was walking to school one day when it started to rain. A school friend and her mother stopped to offer her a ride. The mother invited Holly to her church. When Holly said she already went to a church, the woman inquired, "Where?" When Holly told her, the woman said she should not go there, for the minister was a bad one, causing a lot of trouble and leading people astray.

Holly did not mention her father was the pastor.

Angelyn, our middle child, answered the phone one day and a voice said, "Tell that S.O.B. he had better watch his back," and hung up. The children did learn the tension of living in a community of varying viewpoints.

The Road Less Traveled
Taking a stand on an issue is important for a pastor, but it must be done with great care, for inevitably the issue becomes primary. If this happens, the minister's main task, telling the story of God and God's love that extends to all, will take a backseat. It is crucial that, when a pastor takes a stand, it is consistent with the love of God being for all people. Even with careful evaluation and intentional planning and choices, the minister must be aware of the great need to connect the stand and the message of the gospel.

Unfortunately, many people will only consider the stand, and if they don't see eye-to-eye with the minister, the chance for further ministry with that person is limited. However, as it alienates some, it will cause others to use the stand to re-evaluate their own perceptions of the issue. And many others will be encouraged to take heart and speak up on an issue they have only ever cared about in silence.

While this was going on in Norwood, I once again turned to the seminary and Dr. Tilson for guidance. Taking a stand can cause self-doubt. When self-doubt enters the picture, and angry letters and words are the order of the day, it is crucial to have one or more persons outside the immediate setting to test one's own well-being. It was important for me then, and still is today, to have trusted confidantes within reach to share my experiences. I listened closely to their observations and feedback as I navigated through tense times. Dr. Tilson was willing to share candid thoughts with me—sometimes ones I didn't want to hear.

Then, too, it is important to understand that religious teaching is often not the first thing that comes to a church person's mind when dealing with the issues of life. We are people made by God, but we must remember God formed us from the earth. Matters of the earth and our survival and well-being are our first priority. But God also breathed into us the breath of life. God's Spirit dwells within us. I have discovered that church people eventually remember this truth.

Justice Wins the Day

When I was a district superintendent, I was to introduce a black pastor to an all-Caucasian rural church. Introductions take place with the Staff Pastor Parish Relations Committee for the purpose of determining if there is any reason this person couldn't have an effective ministry at the church.

I prepared myself to remember that, on this Committee, were people made of the earth, and earth matters were the first things that would come to their minds. I reminded myself I needed to wait and not push the Spirit but field the concerns until the Spirit surfaced in their thinking.

The early comments were indeed survival comments. "I am okay with the appointment," one person said, "but my parents are older and will not be able to accept this. At this time they need the church more than ever. I am afraid for them."

"I am concerned this pastor's family might not be safe in the rural setting," said another.

"What if people with children leave, and we lose the opportunity with their children?" someone else said. "We need everyone to survive. If we lose even one family, we would be in trouble, let alone more than one family."

For one hour, they fired their comments. The opposition mounted. Up to this point, I had been listening. I had not gone on the offensive, but I was prepared to if this line of expression went much further.

I kept looking and waiting for their religious teaching to surface. Finally, an older gentleman who had not yet spoken said, "I have been going to this church for over sixty years. I drive by several other churches to get here."

Fear gripped me. If he expressed dissent, this was all over.

"I may have to leave this church," he stated.

Please God, I thought, where are you?

He continued. "I have gone to Sunday School, revival meetings, and sat through several pastors. For years the message has been consistent: all are God's children. Now, I have been thinking, if we say 'no' to this person of color, I might as well stop at one of the other churches. Because, if we say no, we need to hang a sign on our church saying we do not believe what we have been teaching. Right now, tonight is our moment. We are being tested. Are we God's people or not?"

Thank you, Jesus.

The courage of that man immediately helped others remember who they were. The conversation turned to how to best help the new pastor get started.

Two years later, their pastor was on the local school board, and a nearby rural church asked if he could serve their church also. The pastor served there effectively for sixteen years before being appointed to another church.

No Storm Lasts Forever
When one chooses to take a stand, expect the storm clouds to gather, but that is neither a confirmation nor denial of the stand. One must wait for the rainbow. It may take years for the rainbow to appear but, if the stand is consistent with the message of God, then all you need to do is hold on in the storm and wait patiently for a new day.

In the time the ninety letters were printed and answered in the Grace Church newsletter, additional letters appeared in the local paper, *The*

Norwood Enterprise, and no one left the church. Having been there nine years was an important factor, and knowing the people helped.

There was one man who sort of left. He told me that, if I ever let a Black person preach, he would walk out. I did, and he did.

These kinds of people are a gift to a pastor. You know right where they stand. You can count on them. It is the lukewarm ones who wait to see how the battle is going. Then, in the middle of the battle, you realize they are no longer there.

George Morgan walked out the Sunday I had a Black pastor preach, but he was back in several weeks.

"Glad you are here," I said to George after worship. "I thought you had walked out."

"I did," he replied, "but I did not say I was going to stay out."

Three months later, George joined one of the mission trips to Haiti. I have several pictures of him holding Haitian children in his arms. I discovered, in the midst of gruffness, was sometimes a tender heart.

Chapter 14

When I was appointed to Lebanon Church, I immediately became concerned that, in this beautiful, quaint community, I might become a caretaker or chaplain rather than being a part of growth, change, and spiritual development as in my previous appointments.

The first Sunday confirmed my fears, but a door also opened to some interesting possibilities. One was a children's choir with 50 children, six years of age and under. The church also had a preschool where I was able to learn a whole lot about the teaching and nurture of children.

Let the Little Children Come to Me
While at Norwood, I had started a time in the worship service for children. They would come to the front for a story or illustration and then go to another part of the church for crafts and Bible learning. I began having Children's Moments once a month, then twice a month.

One Sunday, when Children's Moments was not scheduled, Kevin Wardrep, age seven, spread out on the pew and remained there throughout the service. At the end of the service, I asked if he was feeling okay.

"I feel fine," he said, "except for Children's Moments. If you are going to have them every other Sunday, then I will only come to church every other Sunday."

Kevin had taken a stand, and he made a good point. From that Sunday on, we had Children's Moments every week.

My experience in the preschool at Lebanon, working with what seemed an endless number of children, enhanced my confidence and comfort level in communication with little ones. The preschool teachers welcomed me as a frequent visitor/story teller/reader and guided me as I found my place in relating well to this age group.

It wasn't that I had been uncomfortable around children in the past. In fact, Wende's mother, Agnes, always enjoyed telling the story about hearing a knock on our back door at the Norwood parsonage, which was next door to the church. When she answered the door, she found five-year-old Vanessa Forrest, who asked if "Gwayson" was home and, if so, was he allowed out to play?

The Lebanon Preschool experience was a more formal learning experience for me in sharing the word of God effectively and simply with young children. I'm grateful for that unexpected gift and training.

Rich in Spirit
When I have been assigned to a new setting, I usually explore the neighborhood. My method is drawn from Dr. Charles' fish story. You will discover things on your fifth stroll through the neighborhood that you missed on the other strolls. Walking often and keeping notes helps me know the neighborhood. However, on my first stroll at Lebanon, I made a great, if unintentional, discovery.

The Lebanon United Methodist Church has an affluent congregation and sits on a corner lot. It is a magnificent Georgian-style church with long clear windows and large pillars at the entrance. At the back of the church building is a parking lot, some fifty feet wide. Just across the parking lot sits an African Methodist Episcopal Church.

In 1787, Richard Allen went to a white Methodist Church in Philadelphia. When he was forced to sit in the balcony and refused communion, he walked out of the church and immediately started the AME Church in protest. He rightfully believed that, for that particular Methodist congregation, it would take just too long for their Christian beliefs to kick in.

At the other end of the lot, immediately across from the preschool, was a home that belonged in a third world country like Haiti. The house was unpainted, sagging, and needed lots of attention. Living in that house was an older woman named Granny and a young man

70

named Tiger. I immediately made their acquaintance, and they enhanced my ministry in Lebanon. Their viewpoint of the world was a good balance for my life and a reminder that the world was bigger than the comforts of our pleasant, safe church.

Granny and Tiger seemed eager to develop a friendship, and I soon moved in and out of their home with great ease. They were poor in some respects but rich with love for each other and a zest for life. I never succeeded in figuring out how to make them a part of Lebanon United Methodist Church, but that probably wasn't necessary anyway. They were still an important part of my ministry in Lebanon, and I have a feeling, looking back on it, that they considered *me* an important part of *their* ministry in the community as well.

On several occasions, as members of Lebanon United Methodist Church were willing to taste the vegetables, we had combined worship services with the AME Church. I have discovered you don't need to write an elaborate sermon about the importance of connecting with others who are different from you. If, as a pastor, you just live it out, others will likely follow along. An idea will soon spread throughout the congregation with little preaching needed.

Jesus Says, "Visit the Prisoner."

I stumbled onto this concept in my first appointment at the Haviland Charge. Jim, a young man of 15, was in jail. Jim's father had been in the war and he married Barbara, an English woman. Together they had three children, and then her husband left. Jim lived close to the church and had been arrested for possible breaking and entering. I was encouraged to make a call on him at the county jail.

I made the call and then asked for a meeting with the Sheriff. I remembered from seminary that pastoral calling required more than a quick call and a prayer. One must take time to get to know the person. Talking through the bars with Jim had great limitations, especially with a deputy standing nearby saying, "Five minutes left." The most unproductive situation involves speaking on a phone through a glass barrier. Many jails will let ministers meet across a table from a prisoner in a secure room, but usually alternative arrangements require prior clearance.

The Sheriff was willing to meet with me, and I asked him to lock me in the cell with Jim for at least four hours. When he denied my request, I went to the Judge. The Judge said my request was interesting and would probably be productive, but the Sheriff was in charge of the jail, not him. On the spur of the moment, I asked the Judge if he would be willing to release Jim to my custody and to our home. He said he would think about it and make the decision the next day.

I was glad for the delay, as I needed to have a conversation with Wende, whom I had obviously not consulted beforehand. She agreed, and together we awaited the Judge's decision.

Jim moved into our home the next afternoon. He was with us for one month at which time the Judge agreed for him to move back with his mother. I do not readily recommend this to all pastors, but I do know news travels fast in church circles, and many people offered money and other help. It provided a wonderful teaching moment.

In the Toledo appointment, a similar situation developed with a young person in jail. The Judge, in that case, was a member of the congregation and gave his immediate approval for me to be locked up with a sixteen-year-old for four hours. This young man taught me how to play Crazy 8's, and the four hours went by rapidly.

I do not know what happened to my Crazy 8's teacher, but Jim married Jane and together they had four children. Jim and Jane show up regularly in our lives, and the relationship has been filled with great meaning.

Perhaps Another Prodigal Son
Paul Farley hailed from Biddeford, Maine. He was a person with a great deal of personality but lacked the knowledge of how to put life together. I met him through one of the Monroe Street youth, Ingrid Gunderson. The youth group went to the Toledo State Hospital each week to play games and engage in conversation with patients. Ingrid had met Paul there and, when he was released, he began attending Monroe Street UMC somewhat sporadically. He would show up, be

around for several months, and then be gone, only to show up again months later.

Some years after that, he had written some bad checks and was being pursued when he again disappeared. I could honestly tell the authorities I had no idea where he was.

Then one day he called from Oregon. He was ready to come home.

"Are you ready to turn yourself in?" I asked.

"Yes," he said, "I want to get this over with, but I need to get back there from Oregon. Is there any way you could send me bus or plane fare?"

"How did you get out there?" I asked.

"A lot of ways," he said. "Got some rides, busses, hitch-hiked."

"Well, you come back using your ability," I told him. "You don't need my bus or plane fare. I am confident, if you got yourself out there, you can get yourself back. I'll start looking for you in four or five days, and I will go with you to turn yourself in."

In four days, he was sitting on the front church steps and I went with him the next day to the police station.

When Paul was released, he got a job as a bartender at the Golden Lamb Restaurant & Inn in Lebanon. The Golden Lamb's lobby boasts photos of presidents who have dined there. Rooms are named after the presidents who stayed in them. Paul became an instant hit at the restaurant. With his personality, his New England accent, and his endless stories, he made many friends. He married, and together he and Betsy had a son, Will.

Then he was told he had a brain tumor that was soon to take his life.

Paul's, and now Betsy's, friends in the community hosted a benefit dinner to help pay some of the medical expenses. Tickets were $25. The hall was packed, and I witnessed an outpouring of human generosity and love that will always remain with me. It was not a church or even churches—it was the whole community. Having experienced the whole story, I imagined it was like the prodigal son and the party his father held when he came home.

Few there knew the story, but they had come to know and love Paul, and tragedy was about to take his life. The Golden Lamb provided the food. Friends decorated the room. Many of the businesses sold tickets. When I went, I was thinking 50 people might show, 75 tops. There were more than 250 people!

Someone had donated two gold pieces worth close to a thousand dollars. They were being raffled off. Most bought the tickets. Many people stood to speak of his life and generous personality. Then it was time for the drawing for the gold pieces. The person who had the number drawn had her ticket on the table but it had mysteriously disappeared.

"Someone must have picked it up when the table was cleaned." Her voice was quivering, and she seemed panicked.

The announcer agreed to give her ten minutes to find the ticket. Several went with her to sort through the trash. Alas, the ticket was not found, and the Master of Ceremonies said another ticket must be drawn.

"And the winner is…" cried the announcer, "…Paul Farley!"

There was a standing ovation as he and Betsy, carrying Will, went to receive the two gold coins. As Paul was accepting the coins, the Master of Ceremonies leaned over and said something to him. I then saw Paul confer with Betsy, and the Master of Ceremonies said, "Paul has accepted an offer to auction off the coins."

So, a quick auction proceeded, and the coins went to the highest bidder at $2200. Again the people stood and cheered.

Several months later it dawned on me. The whole thing was staged. This community I thought might be too quiet and serene for me knew how to love each other and have a great time together. All they needed was a cause—someone dying of cancer.

Now, whenever I think of Lebanon and the endless antique shops, the Golden Lamb and Ice Cream Parlor, I am reminded of the great wealth of love pent up in human hearts, just waiting to be set free.

Chapter 15

If you'll remember from the beginning of the book, a woman came into my office in tears confessing an affair. She and her husband were respected members of our church community. I had found myself attracted to her on a continuing basis, and now she was discussing her sexuality with me. Past fantasies danced around the edges of our conversation. Then, if you'll recall, I ended up at her home, sitting on her couch, her hand on mine, sweating with nervousness and excitement.

I was in a danger zone.

This was long before the time pastors were called together for Sexual Ethics Workshops. Sexual harassment was a term yet to be coined. There were hints now and then of a pastor being moved because of involvement with a parishioner, but those things were talked about in hushed tones, if at all.

I walked out of her house that day, relieved I had escaped without acting on my fantasy. I would love to report that my Bible Club teaching kicked in, along with my lessons from home and the strict sexual understanding of the West Liberty Community. Or perhaps I'd been reflecting on the value of ordination or the long-term values of clergy.

Unfortunately, nothing quite so noble happened. Company arrived just in time. Once they were introduced to me, I made a quick exit.

Humbly Asking for Help
I knew I needed to take some time to ponder this aspect of pastoring a church. The whole experience had jolted me. When I got back to classes, I quickly set up an appointment with Arthur Foster, professor of Pastoral Counseling. I poured the story out to him—my fantasies, my fears, the perspiring, and my narrow escape.

Dr. Foster listened to the whole story. I wondered if he might question my ministerial credentials (those I had) and suggest a halt to further pursuit of clergy status.

Instead, he pointed out some things that had never crossed my mind.

"Human beings are complicated," he said. "We are a mixture of so many things. We think we remember, but the reality is we also forget much of what has happened in our lives. There is a poignant line in the play *Pavilion,* written by Craig Wright, where the narrator asks, 'Is it what we remember that informs life, or what we forget?' So never think that, in any situation, you have before you all the dynamics of your make-up."

"You have told me you have had fantasies of this person. I'm glad you are willing to recognize that, to put it out on the table where you can call it by name and work toward a solution. When the object of a pastor's fantasy presents herself, as you experienced, the pastor has two choices. He can act on the fantasies or choose to be the person's pastor, a stabilizing force in her life."

"But let me be very clear. You cannot be both."

"I invite you to think about your choices. Let's say you use the occasion to act on the fantasy, and start a relationship with her. At first, you may find it exciting and thrilling, but you will need to work out times you can meet together secretly. She will need to keep the information from her family, and you will need to do the same. You will discover that the emotion and effort will take its toll on your ministry. If your relationship is discovered, that will take a great toll on your effectiveness as a pastor. What if one of you loses interest before the other? This could get messy."

"On a positive note, you are not trying to hide your sexuality. Fantasy can be a wonderful part of being human, but often, when we act on a fantasy, the reality becomes something entirely different."

"You must understand that she came to you because of your position. Had you not been appointed to that church you would not have encountered her. You are not just another person; you represent the presence of God in that community to her. To pull that off, you must recognize your gifts as well as your vulnerabilities."

The session soon ended. Dr. Foster had a class to teach, but he had given me a great gift to take back to the church I was serving. I am wondering what it would have been like if the resources had not been there. It was a reminder that understanding myself was my seminary project. Only then could I most effectively be a pastor.

The next day I asked for a recommendation of a psychiatrist. It had become clear to me that, if my life was going to intersect with the lives of others for the next thirty or forty years, I would need as much understanding about myself as was available. That proved to be a valuable experience, and it repeated itself at several points during my 47 years of active ministry.

The Bishop's Advice
This wasn't the only time this tendency toward indiscretion has swirled around my life, but I have discovered a few things over the years.

For one, our society believes one way and often acts another. No couple has ever come to me to marry them without declaring they would be monogamous for as long as they both shall live.

However, I have discovered this is not always how life plays out.

Many times we hold a belief while acting in a way inconsistent with that belief. Nevertheless, the belief never wavers. I don't recall ever talking to someone in the midst of an affair who emphatically supported all affairs. Yet, they justify their own.

A person might say, "I am totally against intimate relationships outside of marriage or partnership, but if others truly knew my situation, they would understand why what I'm doing is okay."

If you ask me, this duality of belief is a result of what I would call evil and the person's mind playing tricks on him or her. It's as if they hold their belief in suspension and convince themselves they are a justifiable exception to the rule.

A relationship between a pastor and a member of the congregation can happen so quickly, primarily because the pastor is involved in the emotional aspects of a parishioner's life. These emotional ingredients are similar to the ones that make up an affair.

I am a bit hesitant to give one bishop's advice, because one might hear it and use it as a license. That was not at all this Bishop's intention. His advice came at a time when we had worked with several pastors in several places who had become involved with someone in their church.

"Never, ever become involved with a member of the congregation," he said. "You are in a unique and vulnerable position of power. To become involved is to violate your position as pastor. But above all, do not become involved with two or more people. If the church is successful in facilitating true community, then, sooner or later, persons involved with you will be in a group together, and the truth will come out. The pastor will be the recipient of great wrath, and a great upheaval will ensue.

"Just remember: as a pastor, you are constantly right at the edge of intimacy. It is your responsibility to be the guardian of the congregation's well-being as well as your own. You may be tempted, and at times parishioners may be tempted to seek inappropriate comfort from you, but it is your job to make sure those boundaries are never crossed by either party."

Chapter 16

For six years, I was a District Superintendent and responsible for 88 churches and 70 pastors. I was part of a group of 14 in similar positions who had knowledge of over 1200 churches and 1000 pastors. I began to understand, in a new way, the shortcomings and great gifts of ministers.

In my first 24 years in ministry, from time to time, I had heard of pastors making unhelpful decisions in relationship with situations and parishioners. Now that I was in an administrative position, I was made aware of each story that surfaced and the involvement that unfolded.

It was a heavy responsibility to have all this knowledge of relationships and ineptness, complaining, outright selfishness on the part of some pastors, and sometimes unreasonable demands of some congregations. And this information was mixed in with the sacrifice of many pastors and extensive love and graciousness of many congregations. This reality brought a new dimension to my understanding and appreciation for the church.

One of my colleagues, Len Confar, likened it to admiring a beautiful set of unlined drapes. Then you stand behind them and see the seams, the hanging threads, the splicing. It does not diminish the beauty but provides another viewpoint that enhances the beauty.

It was in the midst of this experience that a slow process of change began to develop in my own outlook.

One discovery was this: there were a lot more pastors who *said* they wanted to relocate than pastors who were *willing* to move when the call came.

In September, October, and November each year, I would talk with pastors individually. Some would say they were interested in a new appointment, and I would make note of that. Then in January,

February, and March, if there was a place for a person to move, I would go back and say, "We have a place for you," and the pastor would say, "Did I say I wanted to move?"

I began to doubt my ability to listen and accurately record what a pastor said.

What was happening here?

I believe that, in the fall, mentally there was a genuine desire to move, but in the spring, when the door for a move swung open, the pastor's reluctance and denial set in. It was now not a mental decision but reality. We are reluctant to leave the security of what we know for the insecurity of what we do not yet know.

We Were Created for a Place
I have discovered most of us are looking for a place. As children we looked for it under a card table where we threw a blanket over the top. We looked for it on the playground or a ball team or with a teacher, a playhouse, a special place in the back of the closet, or in a loft.

As we move out in life, that longing never leaves us. We say we want a place in the woods or we have a place at the lake or we always wanted a place in the mountains. The need runs deep within our being. If you want to invite a person living alone for Thanksgiving dinner, do not say to them, "If you don't have any place to go, come join us." They will not be there. Tell them you are reserving a place at the table just for them, and if they do not come, then there will be an empty chair. They may not be there, but make no mistake, they know they have a place. That invitation will hang around their life for a long time.

If you are in the home of a friend overnight, and they say "we cleaned up Junior's room and you can sleep in his bed, and he will sleep on the couch," that's okay, but if they are able to take you to a bedroom and announce, "This is the guest room, and it is all yours for tonight," then a place has been provided.

Three blocks from our home in West Liberty was the White Bridge. It had high curved arches and many hiding places. Often, at night, I would climb the arch and sit or lie down on the arch warm from the day's sun. When my Mother died, on the morning of her funeral, I went to The White Bridge, took a good stone and marked a cross on one of the arches. One day they came and tore it down and, in its place, there are two guardrails.

A few years later I was in the home of the Smucker Sisters. They spun their own wool, made their clothing and shoes, and they were artists. On the wall hung a painting of The White Bridge. I moved close to the painting, touched the arches, looked for the hiding places, and then I asked, "Is that painting for sale?"

"Yes, it is," was the reply.

"I'll take it," I said.

"Don't you want to know the price?"

"No, I will take it whatever the price is."

Today that painting hangs on my wall as a reminder of a place I once had.

We all had a place one time. It was the best place anyone could ever have. We were warm, fed, and closer to another human being than we have ever been. That special place was our mother's womb. Nine months later, we were born into this world and whacked on the bottom to start our breathing. The room was cold, the lights were bright, and we began to cry.

"Feed that child!" someone said. "The baby is hungry!"

Hungry! That may be true, but I wonder if we were crying because we had lost our place, and all of our life we look for it, try to find it again. I think that experience is ever with us and shows up when we leave high school and college, move from one place to another. We lost our place once, and we do not want that to happen again.

Folks say older people do not want to go to a care center. What they actually don't want is to once again lose their place. Whether we remember infancy or birth experiences, the reality that we lost our place makes an impact throughout our life.

I believe this losing of our place is at the heart of pastors wanting to move but then losing their nerve when the time comes. Will the next place be better than the one we have now, or will we feel the ache of losing our place?

Jesus told his disciples in John, "I go to prepare a place for you." It may be that, in the end somewhere sometime, we will get our best place back again. The God who made the original plan for us will perhaps make another place just as wonderful as the first, and we will not have to look any longer.

Have We Lost Sight of God's Economy?
As District Superintendent I, along with the Bishop and other Superintendents, had oversight of more than 200,000 people. Each of the pastors related to a community of people, and our task was to match pastors and churches with a goal of effective ministry. A good match would have the possibility of spreading the Good News of God's love for all. Along with every move there were lives interrupted and changes that would have far-reaching consequences.

Many times it was obvious that a certain opportunity would make a tremendous impact on the church. What if we could suddenly match churches and pastors considering only abilities and skills and nothing else? The reality is there are other required considerations—money, salary, location—that made matching skills with need take a back seat. Something seemed terribly broken about this decision-making process when we were relating to One who walked this earth and never had a home or an income. But, with Christ's followers, a predetermined amount was provided monthly with medical insurance, pension, a house, and other benefits.

The reality is we cannot live like Jesus lived, but at the same time, clergy and laypersons are encouraging people to be followers of Jesus. What goes? Are there some ways to follow Jesus today that might resemble the real Jesus? What about that God Spirit within us trying to get noticed, to have some say?

What if, for even one appointment year, the needs of the world could be responded to by those who possessed the personality and skills? And it is not only the church that could be transformed. Look what would happen to the sick, hospitals, the educational system. Must the marketplace and personal needs prevail in the church also?

Is there a possibility we, the church, could once again hear the drum beat and sing together "earthly pleasures vainly call me, I would be like Jesus"?

How Much Do We "Need"?
One day a drama was played out in my office that would have a big impact on my understanding.

If we are watching a play, and find ourselves face-to-face with truth and understanding, it is not because we are learning something new. We are deeply moved, because we are experiencing something we already know, and it is unfolding before our eyes.

Four of the pastors had made appointments with me on the morning of the same day. The appointments were set for 8:00, 9:00, 10:00, and 11:00 am. The first pastor's salary and benefit package was $36,000. In essence, he told me if I could get him an appointment where he could have a package of perhaps $38,000-39,000, he would be in great financial shape.

The next appointment was of a similar nature, only this pastor believed, if a package of $41,000-42,000 were available, it would help put life together as presently there was a financial struggle. This pastor's present salary was what the first pastor was hoping for.

The third appointment was a similar request. He and his wife had been experiencing a financial squeeze. If I could get him moved to a place where the salary was $44,000-45,000, it would really make a difference. This pastor's present salary was what the second pastor was hoping he might receive.

Before the fourth pastor came in, and since it seemed like money was the order of this day, I looked up her package and it was $25,000. She wanted to talk with me about two things: continuing education and an invitation to me to preach at the church she served. Before she left, I asked how she was getting along financially.

"I am making more now that I ever have," she said, "and, in fact, I have more than I need."

Some things in life one needs to file away for future reference. That morning was filed away in my memory.

The reason I wanted to keep that four-appointment morning close by was simply because there are some things that clergy consider to be clergy rights. They are viewed as essential and reasonable, a primary consideration in the appointment making process.

But when we have claimed that right and expect that right, haven't we given up a beautiful aspect of people called by God to a needy world and sold it for a mess of potage?

A Pastor Does the Right Thing
Having all this in mind, there was a church in a small community that seemed on the edge of considerable growth. The church had become open because the pastor was retiring. He had been a good pastor, a steady plodder, but lacked creativity and vision. There was a pastor who could be moved from a mostly rural setting where the potential was somewhat limited.

When I proposed that pastor for the open church, it was pointed out that the salary was $2,000 less than he was presently receiving. I insisted this was an ideal match. There was considerable resistance. Pastors occasionally accepted a salary decrease, but it was usually the result of a lack of skills or some kind of failure at their previous appointment. A pastor with excellent skills and a clean record was never suggested as a "great match" if it came with a decrease in salary. That would be "unfair" and "you wouldn't want to do that to a family."

But now, following the drama in my office, I had been thinking about this whole matter for some time, and so I was prepared with well-crafted arguments in favor of this appointment. I was just waiting for the right moment. Finally I was given permission to talk with the pastor to see if he was willing to take a pay cut. Honestly, the appointment was oozing with opportunity without any adjustments.

I met with the pastor, and he was willing. This didn't surprise me as I sensed a high level of commitment from him up to this point in our conversations.

But I was not prepared for what happened when I took him for the introduction. The Staff Parish Relations Committee was very skeptical of someone willing to take a pay cut. They did not offer to raise the salary and came very close to saying, no.

The pastor and spouse went into the sanctuary while I continued the conversation with the committee. To be willing to accept a decrease in salary was one thing. To be hesitant, questioning, and unwelcoming was not expected. Upon reflection, though, I might have had that reaction myself had I been in their place.

The Committee was finally willing to go along with the appointment. When I went into the sanctuary to speak with Mark and Melinda, there were tears and second thoughts. Why wouldn't there be? In their present appointment, they were both beloved.

What I learned that evening was that, when you do the daring and creative thing, it does not mean people will call you blessed. You need to be ready for many other possibilities. In the midst of the reluctance and resistance, it became tempting to doubt the decisions.

The match worked. Several months later, on a Sunday morning, I stopped at that church for worship. I attempted to slip in and be seated. I quietly opened the door, spotted an empty seat and sat down. The church was packed. Much to my surprise I had gone in the choir entrance and I was seated with the choir. While I was in the process of deciding what to do, the choir stood for the anthem, so I stood with them and lip-synced my way through a wonderful arrangement of Amazing Grace.

That was my first and last Sunday as part of their choir, but Mark spent eleven years as their pastor, and they flourished.

The Confederate Flag Dance
It was my intention to have a conversation with each pastor every year, either in my office or at the church they were serving.

On my visit with one pastor, I was taken back when I entered his office. He had a Confederate flag displayed on his desk.

I decided not to make the flag the first topic of conversation. I asked about the church, his family, and asked him if there were any issues or concerns he wanted to share with his District Superintendent.

About a half hour into our conversation, I asked about the Confederate flag on his desk.

"A symbol of the South," he said, "and I am a product of the South. I spent my early years in Kentucky."

"Are you aware," I asked, "that the Confederate flag is considered quite controversial by many people? Many white people and most black people are offended by it because of the past it represents."

"Well, there are no black people at this church" he offered cheerfully, "and I really can't help it if some are offended by its presence."

"Well," I said, choosing my words carefully, "people come into your office for counseling and when they come, there is a possibility they might be turned off immediately over the display of the flag."

"Well, it seems to me that is their problem, not mine."

I turned to another subject. I needed some time to decide if I would pursue this discussion of the placement of this flag or drop the matter.

Finally I said, "You seem to be a good pastor wanting to do a good job. I am concerned about the flag on your desk and the possibility of it interfering with your effectiveness."

"Are you offended by it being on my desk?" he asked.

"A bit," I said, "I am offended and uneasy about why it is important to you to have it there."

"How can I help you get over that?" he asked.

"Well," I replied, "would you be willing for you and I to meet with three other pastors and get their ideas on the subject? We could see if this is just my issue or if there might be a broader concern."

"I would be willing," he replied. "When do you have in mind?"

"How about if you share with me the names of three pastors you trust the most, and I will get us all together." He agreed.

Three weeks later we met with the ministers that he had suggested. One of them was a close colleague of mine, and I knew him to be open and progressive on civil rights issues. I related the story of entering the office and seeing the Confederate flag and then said, "I would like to ask each of you to give your reflection on this matter."

Each pastor responded. The responses were polite, but they did not give much affirmation to the display of the Confederate flag on a pastor's desk. Nor did they definitively advise him to remove the flag. One pastor said he would not display anything that might be a hindrance to someone seeking help. This was the most direct and helpful thing that was said, and I left the meeting unsure if my "peer review" experiment had been successful.

I was curious, but I never went back in his office again to see if the flag was still there. I later recalled that he had one of those Doctor of

Ministry degrees and his doctoral thesis was focused on the dynamics of grief counseling. Maybe he was just drumming up clients, but I always hoped the ministers he had selected for feedback had planted a seed of some sort with him.

Chapter 17

In 1986, the first woman became a district superintendent in the 18th year of the West Ohio Conference.

Two other conferences had appointed women superintendents. Bishop Ammons told us he felt it was time, if not past time, to have a woman on the Cabinet.

I put this story here because it is a microcosm of the dynamics involved in change. And, although our conference now takes women district superintendents for granted, it was the courage and passion of Bishop Ammons that made it happen.

All in Favor
When Bishop Ammons made the announcement, it was received with great enthusiasm. Several superintendents said they had been thinking the same thing. One spoke to offer his view that it was typical of Bishop Ammons to be out in front of other conferences and to take the lead to bring about change.

Another said, "This will encourage women pastors, and they will feel fully represented with a woman on the Cabinet."

In the following hour-long discussion, not one word of opposition surfaced.

"This will be a new day for all of us, and it will be thrilling to be a part of this change," many said. This sentiment was expressed in various ways during the entire hour.

So Bishop Ammons brought the discussion to a close by asking all of us to come up with the name of one woman from our district for consideration.

On Second Thought

At the next Cabinet meeting, no one brought up the subject until the Bishop asked for each superintendent's suggestion.

"Well, I thought I had the perfect candidate," one superintendent said, "but then it occurred to me that she has difficulty driving at night." In his mind, this eliminated her from consideration.

Another superintendent said that, although there were several female pastors in his district, he could not offer any of them as a candidate.

Another spoke up saying that a significant number of churches had indicated they would not accept a woman pastor. "We all know this is wrong," he said, "but imagine a woman superintendent taking a woman pastoral candidate to a church. There would be dynamics set in motion keeping the candidate from having a fair chance."

The Bishop replied, "Now let me understand. You're saying we should not appoint a woman superintendent, because we might lessen the chance of a woman being appointed to a church?"

"Well, yes," the superintendent said, "but if the church is negative to women in leadership positions, then even if she is introducing a male candidate, it might interfere with his acceptance at that church."

"So, let me ask you," the Bishop said, "If a church has an unfounded bias against women in leadership, are you indicating we should let our actions be determined by that church bias?"

This was getting good, and I couldn't help but wonder how it would end.

"Well," the superintendent replied, "I, myself, do not feel that bias should be the main factor, but it is a factor and people need a chance to change."

"And aren't we giving them that chance by providing an opportunity to confront their bias?"

92

The Bishop was not backing down.

"Well, that all sounds good, but the reality is many of these people have no intention of changing."

The Bishop continued. "Would you say that, across the board, committees have this mindset? Might there be some committees who will be energized and come alive with an opportunity like this?"

"Well, perhaps," the superintendent said, "but don't count on the women to be the ones energized, because some of the women are the most prejudiced against women pastors."

Another superintendent had been trying to speak, and the Bishop recognized him.

"I want you to know I am all in favor of the direction we are moving," he began. "However, I want to remind us of the overall parameters we have always used in selecting superintendents. First, the church the person is presently serving. Has it provided the administrative challenge that will come to a superintendent? Most of the women are serving smaller churches that could not possibly equip a pastor to step into the superintendency. What if we make a woman a superintendent and she fails because of the lack of preparation? I am sure we all want this first woman to succeed, not fail."

"Secondly, pastors becoming superintendents usually get a bump in salary of $5,000, $10,000, even $15,000. There is not one woman presently serving who would fall into that category. Presently the highest-paid woman would receive a $17,500 increase, and she has several children and could not possibly fill the role of superintendent, so that leaves others where the salary jump would be the biggest in history. Do you think we might be creating a morale problem among other pastors?"

"Well, you have a point there," the Bishop said.

We all noticed he did not say you have a *good* point or *weak* point. He simply said, "You have a point."

The Bishop Speaks His Mind

"We will discuss this more at our next Cabinet meeting," the Bishop said. "I ask you to continue thinking about women who would fit well into the position. I also ask you to lay aside what other people would think or do, or how they would perceive this action. We cannot operate on the basis of how some people might act. We do not ultimately have control over that."

"Further, I want you to keep in mind that, when we participate in change and when the moment calls for action, then the old guidelines, ways, and patterns become a hindrance rather than a help."

"If we decide it is time to take the step of appointing a woman, then we must boldly take that step. I am convinced we must set aside the old guidelines of church size and salary and family make-up and focus on the change that needs to take place. I enlist all of you to get on board with this bold moment of forward progress."

Soon the decision was made and, in a short time, the first woman, Gail Rohrbacher, took her seat at the Cabinet table. It was a profound moment and a great gift of the West Ohio Conference. Gail Rohrbacher served with distinction.

That was in 1986. Over the 26 years since then, 11 women have served on the West Ohio Cabinet.

Thank you, Bishop Edsel Ammons.

Chapter 18

It is one thing to profess high ideals of how ministry should work. It's another to actually live it out in your own life.

"What if, for just one year," I wrote earlier, "every pastor would be willing to be sent where most needed, where their skills match needs without thought of salary, parsonage, size of church, etc.?"

Serving as a district superintendent means gaining knowledge and confidence and enjoying a generous salary. When one's term is up, the subsequent church appointment is typically commensurate.

One day, as the superintendents were meeting with the Bishop, I turned to George Brown who sat beside me. George was a funny man, mostly because he could deliver one-liners with a straight face.

Once when the Bishop asked why it was important to take a Discipline to all charge conferences, George replied that he never took a Discipline to charge conferences. When asked why by the Bishop, George with no trace of a smile, said, "I find taking a Discipline limits my options."

That day I turned to George and said, "Just tell me, George. Just tell me so I can understand. Why must we forever make appointments based on salary and size?"

It was not the first time George heard this question from me. Since he sat beside me, I often made these comments to him rather than risking the thought with the whole group.

"How long have you been a district superintendent?" he asked.

"Five years," I replied.

"Well, next year, try it out with your appointment and see how it plays out. Do it yourself if it means that much to you."

That day George planted a seed. In a very quiet, innocent way he had instructed, "Why don't you stop belly aching about the issue and do it yourself?"

It was a major moment. For the next six months I worked on my speech. Without the struggle that had taken place, George's suggestion would have fallen on deaf ears. Often it seems we have good ideas for others but not necessarily ourselves.

A Lesson From My Daughter

Our youngest child, Holly, had provided a story from her life that, for some time, had complimented my thinking. When we lived in Norwood, a Baptist Church in the northern part of Cincinnati hung an advertisement on our parsonage door about Summer Bible School. By calling the church, a bus would come by each night and pick up any child interested. Holly, eight at the time, asked if she could call. We gave our consent.

The first night we watched as the bus arrived, and she climbed on and took a seat by the window. At that point, she was the only one on the bus. Holly was rather shy, and we felt this adventure might be helpful to her.

Each night she met the bus and returned about 9:30 p.m. She had clearly enjoyed herself. But, on the last night, she ran in the house, went straight to bed, and cried herself to sleep. All efforts to get her to speak of her pain were to no avail.

Ten years later, on a weekend home from college, she shared her story with us. She related how, on the first night, and each of the following nights of the Bible School, each child was asked to write his or her name on a piece of paper and drop it in a big box at the front of the sanctuary. On the last night, a drawing would take place for the world's biggest Hershey's bar. Each night she had dropped in her name and dreamed of taking the world's biggest Hershey's bar home to her family.

On the last night, when it was finally time for the drawing, Holly said the mood in the sanctuary was electric. A man with a deep voice put his hand in the box and took a long time drawing out a name. When he finally opened the piece of paper, he squinted, and paused and then, in a booming voice said: "Holly At-Ha."

Holly started to get up but realized the pronunciation was wrong on her last name. Then she wondered if it even was her name. She wasn't sure what to do. Meanwhile, the announcer kept calling her name. Holly wanted to go claim the bar, but the thought of being wrongly accused of not being Holly At-Ha was keeping her glued to her seat. Surely there were teachers and leaders there who knew her and could have spoken up.

No one did.

She sat on her hands, frozen to her seat. The name Holly At-Ha was called over and over again. Finally, another name was drawn, and Holly's dream was shattered. She went home and cried herself to sleep.

When she finally told that story to us, a full decade later, tears still came to Holly's eyes and to ours too.

From that moment on, whenever my name was called, even if it did not sound just like my name, I would listen. If a call were made for help, I would listen. Is it me? Maybe yes, maybe no, but I was not going to miss this opportunity.

Listen closely. Someone may be calling your name.

Putting My Money Where My Mouth Was
"How about you?" George said. At that moment I sensed my name had been drawn, and I walked from the room that day a changed man.

A district superintendent's term was six years. At the end of the term, if the person was not retiring, he or she would be asked to what type of church he or she would like to be assigned. The group would then

97

discuss possible appointments in the person's absence, a decision would be made, and the individual informed.

My moment had arrived. The discussion involved several churches with several hundred members and salaries commensurate with my current salary. In other words, we were headed down the same old appointment-making path.

This wasn't about where I was most needed; it was about who could afford me. Now seemed to be the moment to act, but how?

I really felt my name was being called. And, with sudden clarity, I said, "I want to be appointed to a circuit of churches where the salary is the minimum salary. And, when asked about the appointment, I want the Cabinet to say, "The Bishop appointed Grayson to the place where his talents and abilities could be best used."

It was really not fair to make that request of my colleagues. It was clear to me that the discussion had, of necessity, shifted. The issue was not, at this moment, truly matching abilities and skills; it was about making a statement so that, in the future, the door might open just a bit to allow the appointment-making process to shift in a new direction.

The Bishop, to this point, had been mostly silent. We were used to the long silences and knew that, when he spoke, his words would be wise.

"If one in our midst believes God is calling him to a particular type of assignment," he said, "then we need to be careful lest we ourselves interfere with the call. Right now it is time to break for lunch, and if you have no plans for lunch, Grayson, I would ask you to take lunch with me."

Over lunch he again affirmed the need to consider carefully if we "think" or "hear" a call.

"So, Grayson," he said, "if I appointed you to Mt. Zion Church, would that fit into what you think is your call?"

98

Mt. Zion I knew about. It was an African-American Church about three miles from where I had served in Norwood. Mt. Zion was located in the community people in Norwood had told us not to drive through. If I said yes, we would be living in the community others purposely avoided.

That is one of the great things about the appointive system of the United Methodist Church. It takes you to a place you would have never gone. It opens you to experiences you never would have had.

There is a mystery about the appointive system, for you may end up in a place that will change the direction of your life, your friends, your medical care, and entertainment.

You will potentially emerge a new person altogether.

Unfortunately, some pastors do not sense the potential or opportunity and fight against the assignment for one, or even two, years until it dawns on them that a new world has opened up to them and, in the midst of their complaining, they have missed out.

I must say that, once in a while, an appointment is made that misses the mark. There have been pastors who have made great efforts to make it work, but it seemed it was not to be. And United Methodists have a reputation for being able to change an appointment almost as quickly as they can make one.

Never Give Up
I knew one of the recent pastors at Mt. Zion, Samuel Wright. For years I had heard his speeches on the conference floor at Lakeside, where he spoke on behalf of African-American pastors and churches he felt were being treated shabbily by the conference. Time after time he would rise to plead the case.

One time I remember vividly he spoke directly to a Bishop and said, "There has never been a Black District Superintendent. Are none of us qualified? Who knows? We have asked over and over and over, 'What are the qualifications?' and we have never been told. Maybe, if you tell us the qualifications, then we will see none of us are qualified.

But perhaps someone among us could possibly work to become qualified if indeed we are not now qualified. But, if none of us have ever been appointed, and we do not know what we need to do to *be* qualified, then what hope is there for us?"

Time after time he would address the 3,000 gathered. I thought he would lose heart, but he never did.

His speeches were a judgment on all of us as we just sat there waiting for him to sit down. Sometimes I would remember that the Jackson Family was run out of West Liberty. They were Black, and the community ran them out. Not everyone ran them out, but some did.

And the rest were silent.

In the powerful words of Reverend Martin Luther King, Jr., "History will have to record that the greatest tragedy of this period of social transition was not the strident clamor of the bad people, but the appalling silence of the good people."

I kept saying to myself, "When is your moment?" I was becoming increasingly uneasy. How could I continue to sit there? I knew too much.

When Samuel Wright rose to speak, I could not stay in my seat. I walked up beside him and said in a loud voice, "Sam, sit down. I am making the speech for you today. My seat won't hold me any longer."

I stated what we needed to do as a conference, and what I needed to do as a clergy, and then I ended by saying, "I cannot determine what this conference will do, but I will tell you, if this year I fail to act to change what is, I will not be back next year. I will not set foot in this place again until I act."

When I heard several years later that Samuel Wright was near death, I called and took a tape recorder and four pints of Graeter's Ice Cream. I wanted once again to hear his articulate words and powerful emotion. That was not the right moment, but he asked me to leave the tape recorder, and he would speak into it when his body and emotions were able and willing.

After he died, his wife returned the tape recorder to me. It was blank. I was reminded one does not have endless opportunities to hear the great orators. We must listen while we can.

Back to my lunch meeting with the Bishop. He had asked me a question. He was waiting for my answer.

I told him yes.

Chapter 19

The Bishop told me to talk it over with my family and let him know the next day.

That night the children were called, and Wende and I had a long discussion with each of them. We were all in agreement that I should take this appointment.

The introduction was set up for three weeks from that date and, as often happens, two of the children and Wende began to scout out the area looking for a place to live.

The introduction took place at Mt. Zion Church. There were seven members of the Committee present, the district superintendent, Wende, and I. For all practical purposes, it was a welcoming meeting. In our conference there had been several Black pastors assigned to predominantly White churches but not as many White pastors at Black churches. One of the topics of discussion was if there were any white members of the church. Some on the Committee thought there was one white member, but others thought the white person was the spouse of a black member who really belonged to another church.

I discovered early on that there were many couples in the church who went to two different churches. My experience over the years was that, at the time of marriage, the choice was made, either the church of one or the other or an all-new church setting for both of them. But I was discovering a new level of comfort. If each had grown up in a church, been nurtured in the church, a choice would not have to be made. It was a new experience for me, but it seemed to give a high level of value to the church experience, the church roots as an alternative to yours, mine, or something new.

A physician on the Committee offered a helpful viewpoint for my early days at Mt. Zion. "For years," he said, "whenever a white person showed up in the black community, the question in the minds of the people was 'What does this white person want? What is this person here for?'"

"There was always some reason that was not positive for the black community. You need to be aware that, when you get started here, the first thought will not be 'He is here to be our pastor.' That will come later. So be aware early on that many in the congregation will be wondering why you are here. The question will be answered by how you carry out your ministry."

There was a long pause, and then he continued, "When I was a child, and my Mother was a teacher, she came home one day and gathered all of us children together. She said the school where she taught was proposing to pay black teachers one salary and white teachers another. She said she had called us together to tell us that would not be satisfactory, and all the black teachers would refuse to teach until the salary was made right."

"'Now children,' she continued, 'the days ahead will be hard. We will not have money we need or food we need or clothing we need, but as long as they treat us one way and others another, we black teachers are not going back there.'"

Dr. Bowers continued, "We went through some hard times, but we knew we were part of a cause for Mom and a lot of others, and so we did not complain, because the cause was much bigger than our own needs. When my mother went back to work as a teacher with a salary equal to white people, it was a victory for our family. I was always grateful that our mother let us in on what was going on so we could fully participate."

"Over the years I have thought The United Methodist Church needs to take a stand for what is right. I have thought about it, wondered about it, but this night here in this room had not occurred to me. This is the moment for which I have been waiting. I am ready to get started today."

Ripe for a New Vision

It seems, in every setting, there are those who make a difference. In a way, they are tide turners. They shape the conversation and thinking of those gathered. A lot of negative, pessimistic thought can be redirected by a positive story in testimony. I have often thought the negative viewpoints are not really on solid ground, and those offering them welcome a tide turner. They live in the negative, or in a world of fear of what could happen, and when one offers a new heaven and new earth possibility, then often they are ready to grab hold of that new vision.

I had experienced that so vividly when I introduced a black pastor to a white church in Findlay, Ohio. The Bishop had asked us over and over to think of a white church where we could place a black pastor. Several times I had gone to worship at St. Paul's Church in downtown Findlay. As I sat in worship, looked around into the faces of the people, felt the Christian Spirit around, I then went back to the Cabinet and said, "Bishop, the answer to your question is St. Paul's Church."

Another superintendent who knew something of the churches in the Findlay District said, "That is the last place I would take a black pastor."

"So what is the first church?" I asked.

"I do not really know, but why do you suggest St Paul's?"

"Well, they are a beautiful church, and they have a conservative theology," I said. "They are set on doing what the Bible says. I really think they will be ready to follow the biblical teaching that all of us are God's children. Besides, when I talked to them about the kind of pastor they would like, they said they would like one who really stood out in the community. When people saw their pastor, they wanted them to say, 'Hey, there is the pastor of St. Paul's United Methodist Church.'"

"Since the community is 98% white, I figure a black pastor will quickly be noticed in the community."

At the introduction when the question was raised about the lack of African-Americans in the community, and where the new parsonage family would find family in the community, a member of the Committee quickly spoke up saying, "We all will be their family."

A father of two young sons said he had been wondering how he could help his young sons prepare for a world where there were many African-Americans. He said he had thought and thought about that and never had it occurred to him that the experience could come through his pastor. He declared, "I am ready to get started right now. When will this take place?"

Our New Life Begins

We moved into the Mt. Zion parsonage on a July afternoon. It was a beautiful older home with a wonderful front porch that spread across the whole front of the house. Gifts of food and flowers were brought by as we unloaded our belongings. Our children came from out of town to help us move in, and because the carpet on the second floor had been cleaned and was taking a little longer to dry than estimated, due to the humidity, we all slept on the living room floor that first night—and we couldn't have been happier.

Several days later, a 13-year-old boy named Keith stopped by and asked if we had some time to talk. Keith reported that he had been watching since the day we moved in, and he thought there were some things we needed to know.

"In case you are interested," he said. "There is one other white family in the neighborhood. They live two streets north."

He said he would be glad to introduce us to them if we needed to know any other white people. He reported that our next-door neighbors were Kuwan, who was 10, and Jason, who will ask early on if we have a piano and could he practice on it?

"You will need to decide, but I wanted you to know the request would be coming," Keith continued. He hastened to say that he himself would let Jason practice on his piano if he had one.

"Also, there is this man whose name is Fat Marvin. You can't miss him, because he is quite the opposite of fat. If there is anything you need, you contact me and, if necessary, I will contact the others. We have been talking, and we will all be on call. Now, when the Big Cheese comes, we will be gone, but we will all be back in the late afternoon."

"And who is the Big Cheese?" I asked.

"The school bus," he replied.

Of course.

All four of the children were frequent visitors to the parsonage. Their help and oversight was a valuable experience for Wende and me.

The first Sunday at the church we were received with open arms. The choir was led by Daphne Robinson, who also played the organ. The choir was a gathering of excellent singers, who sang two anthems— one was a gospel number, and the second a traditional hymn choral anthem.

The two anthems on the first Sunday were sung together, and I made a mental note that perhaps the two could be sung at different times. When I later raised the matter with Mrs. Robinson, she said they had considered that, but the choir was made up of older persons who were not in the best physical condition. When they got up to sing one song, it was easier to stay up and do both.

The sanctuary was a beautiful structure with stained glass windows. I had last been in the sanctuary at Rev. Samuel Wright's funeral when it was filled with family and friends including many clergy and persons from public office. There are some church sanctuaries that, when one enters them whether empty or full, the very place gives off a sense of the presence of God. Mt. Zion sanctuary was one that gave you the feeling that "surely the presence of God is in this place."

Finding My Way (with Help)

My first Sunday at Mt. Zion was also the first Sunday of July and, therefore, it was Communion Sunday. The kneeling rail was covered with white cloths as were the pulpit and the pulpit chairs. There were many hats, and Sunday best was the order of the day. There were ushers in white gloves, and the utter dignity of the whole service was refreshing. It was a Sunday I will always remember.

Mt. Zion had an associate minister who had been there for years. The Reverend Miss Clara P. Ruffin was a small woman in her late eighties, very kind, but not timid. She was a real lifesaver for me. I asked her questions about everything, and she was more than helpful.

In any church situation it is good if one has some ideas about do's and dont's. Some folks like to be called on regularly and some don't. I don't ever remember The Reverend Miss Clara P. Ruffin saying a negative thing about anyone, but she was full of information (if asked), and that made getting started so much easier. She was a wonderful colleague.

On the first Sunday I introduced myself and Wende and the family. I shared with the congregation my journey to Mt. Zion and that it was an honor to be received as their pastor. I remembered it is important to be open and vulnerable. I told the congregation I, no doubt, had prejudice lurking around in my life, and I would be on the lookout for it, and asked them to point out any aspects of my ministry they felt were not helpful.

After the service our family was invited to the Fellowship Hall for a reception. There was silver service and great heaps of finger sandwiches. The food and tables were almost straight out of a gourmet magazine. When I commented to a couple of people about the beauty of the spread, they said with a smile, "We have been doing this for years. From where do you think all those finger sandwiches in the world come?"

After the reception, the lay leader, Ernest Mills, asked if I had a few minutes to talk. He went into the office with me and said, if it were okay, he would point out some possible pitfalls from time to time. I assured him I would welcome that.

"In the service you said you no doubt have some prejudices. I know you are trying to be forthright, and that is good, but some might seize the opportunity to hear only part of what you say and tell people you are prejudiced. You might say, 'I am not perfect, but I am working on it and, with your help, perhaps I can move closer to being perfect.' Then secondly, try to eliminate the words 'you' and 'yours' from your vocabulary. Always say 'we' and 'ours.' It is not a big issue, but it will help bring us closer together."

Throughout my time at Mt. Zion, Mr. Mills had several of these talks with me, and I found it an essential component of a cross-racial appointment.

Before starting at Mt. Zion, I had written to most of the African-American pastors in our conference to ask for their advice as I started at Mt. Zion. One writer responded that the congregation would tell me how I was doing—I just needed to understand the language in the Black Church.

"For instance," she wrote, "if someone says to you, 'That was a really good sermon, but we need a bit more gravy,' don't spend time trying to figure out how to change your sermon. The comment is not about the sermon; it's about your pastoral care. You need to do more calling."

Most wrote that, if you are effective in a mostly white church, you use the same skills and you will be okay in a black church.

Chapter 20

Early on I began calling on those who could not come to worship. I met Miss Evelyna Forney Grace, a 90-something resident in a care center in Kenwood. She was a delightful woman who was willing and ready to come to Mt. Zion if she had transportation. So we worked out a transportation team, and most Sundays she was present in her wheelchair at the front of the church. The transportation team soon learned that she usually found a way to smoke on the ride to and from church whether one allowed smoking in their car or not.

The first time she got in my car she asked where the ashtray was. I told her, since I didn't have one, that smoking in the car was really impractical. By this time she had her cigarettes out and said, "I'll go ahead and light up and we can deal with that problem later."

From then on I left an old H&H Diner cup in my car with a little bit of water in it for her to use as an ashtray when she rode with me.

One day I heard she was upset because she had to move from the care center in Kenwood to a different place. I visited her to find out what was going on. I became furious when I discovered the reason. Money had run low, and the care center in Kenwood did not take residents who received Medicaid. I went to the management to complain that this woman in her nineties had become adjusted to this place, had spent all of her money there, and when it ran out, they no longer had a place for her.

The management was nice and apologetic, but some things cannot be changed.

When I left there, and went looking for Miss Grace, I discovered she had already been moved. I drove directly to the new place to console her. I stopped on my way to purchase a carton of cigarettes for her. I seldom did such a thing in my ministry except for those over 90 who had no intention of breaking their habit. She often told me she planned to quit when she died.

When I walked into her room, I had thought of many words of comfort, ways I might help this nice lady adjust to this injustice in our society. Frankly, I brought the cigarettes as a part of my overall attempt to comfort.

When I walked in the room she looked at me and smiled and said, "Well, what do you think?"

"Well," I said in the most positive tone I could muster, "it looks pretty nice."

She called me to her side and, as if it were a secret between the two of us, she said, "This place is a hell of a lot better than Kenwood."

Well, so much for the prepared consolation, and so much for my need to take care of her. She had taken care of herself, thank you very much.

I gave her the cigarettes anyway.

The Power of Presence
It was evening on the second Sunday of my being the pastor of Mt. Zion. I was driving home when I thought of a woman in the congregation who was dying of cancer. I felt compelled to go to her home before I went to mine. She was a woman in her early fifties, a popular teacher well-loved by her high school students. She had been taken from the hospital to her mother's home. When I arrived, I was warmly welcomed and someone took me upstairs to see her. When I entered the room, I knew why I had felt compelled to make the call. Death was imminent.

There is a painting that has always fascinated me; the one of the doctor sitting by the bedside of a child. Adults hover over the bed. The medicine bag is closed as if nothing more can be done. The doctor's presence is powerful. Waiting is a valued action.

So I drew up a chair by the bed and waited. People kept moving in and out of the room. I could hear the sounds of them climbing the steps. Then they were waiting also; the mother, the daughter, students, friends.

Soon after midnight her breathing stopped. She was gone. There was a prayer after all were called around the bed. And soon the funeral director arrived. I asked if we might all gather in the living room and, in a circle, we joined hands and there was another prayer.

Following the prayer, the funeral director asked the Mother, "Would you like for me to call the former pastor and see if he is available for the funeral?"

The Mother walked across the circle, took my hand, and said to the funeral director, "This is my pastor."

In that room, I heard Dr. Bower's words, "At first they will wonder why you are here, but soon they will know you are here to be their pastor."

It had come more quickly than I anticipated.

At the funeral, the grand sanctuary of Mt. Zion was filled. I was the preacher, and Rev. Miss Clara P. Ruffin assisted. We walked down the aisle behind the casket and read the Twenty-Third Psalm with the congregation responding.

The Lord is my shepherd... *I will have no fear.*
The Lord leads me beside green pastures... *I will have no fear.*

That day, I felt as if I had been a part of Mt. Zion all my life. And I felt grateful to have been able to share in these sacred moments with the people there.

The Power of Music
So I made it a point to do the gravy bit early on. Mr. and Mrs. Charles Grayson lived close to the church but seldom attended worship services. Charles Grayson was in the early stages of Alzheimer's, and

Mrs. Grayson worked long hours to keep life together. Mr. Grayson was an accomplished musician and had played the guitar in many places in Cincinnati and in other parts of the country.

"Do you play the guitar anymore?" I asked, on a visit to their home.

"No," he replied.

"How long since you last played?"

"A long time," his wife said. "For two years he has not picked up the guitar."

"Do you still have your guitar?" I asked.

"Yes."

"Would you be willing to play it for me?" I asked. He shook his head no.

"Charles," his wife said, "the pastor has asked you to play the guitar."

I was suddenly aware of the power of the pastor in the Black Church.

Mrs. Grayson left the room and came back with the guitar. Charles opened the case, slowly removed the guitar, hooked up the strap, and put it over his shoulder. I looked at his wife, thinking perhaps I should withdraw the request. She raised her finger to her lips indicating I should hold my ground.

Mr. Grayson began to pick at the guitar. Soon his foot was tapping. He got to a certain place in the song, and he tried several times to get it but it eluded him. Finally, he stopped, took the guitar off his shoulder, patted it several times, and put it back in the case.

I do not know if he ever got his guitar out again.

Even though that brief kitchen table concert was, in no way, equal to his great talent, I sensed Mr. Grayson had once been a great musician on whom age and disease had taken an unfair toll. I experienced something at that table that day, and when I left that house, I felt I had been in a great concert hall where human struggle was vividly played out.

It was a drama etched in my brain that I will never forget.

Children Are Our Future

Mt. Zion was located in the center of a large housing project. I could walk out the church door and soon be in the midst of a multitude of children. Each evening, at about 6:30 p.m., I would walk through the project with large plastic bags and two grabbers. As I made my way around the project, picking up various items of litter, left by those passing through the neighborhood, I would accumulate a gathering of children and many requests for the extra grabber. Sometimes a child would prevail, and I would act as if it was a chore to give up my own grabber.

It proved a very effective way to gather children together.

Pieces of wrapped candy often made their way from my pockets to the ground and were quickly grabbed by laughing children. They loved the part of the game where I acted as surprised as they were.

One day I was leaving the church in a hurry to get to a funeral of a sister of one of our church members. When I opened the church door there stood one of the children with a dead baby squirrel in his hand. He asked if the squirrel could be buried on the church lawn. I told him I needed to get to a funeral but to give me the squirrel and for him to return at 9:00 am the next morning.

I put the squirrel in the church freezer and headed for the funeral. When I arrived I was ushered to the choir loft to be seated with other clergy. I had learned that, at funerals like this, every clergy would be called on to make remarks. I was thinking about what I wanted to say when it hit me. Here was a child with a baby squirrel, asking me if the squirrel could be buried on the church lawn, and I had left the child and rushed off to the funeral. Suddenly, I realized what I had done, and I felt a great need to go back and find the child, but I really could not leave the choir loft without causing a major disruption.

The next morning I went to the church with shovel in hand. The child was there. A hole was carefully dug. The squirrel was wrapped in a white cloth napkin and placed in the newly-dug grave. I asked the child if he would like for me to have a prayer. He said yes.

I bowed my head and thanked God for all the animals of the world and especially for this child with a tender heart and asked that God might continue to touch his life so he would never lose his love and tender care. I peeked at him during my prayer. I learned to do this as a child. It appears your eyes are closed, but you can still see.

What I saw was beautiful. There was the child standing on the grave with head bowed, holding his hat over his heart.

But, in that moment, I noted behind him six other children with their faces pressed against the bars of the iron fence just beyond the grave. I had lamented the church's lack of formal Children's Christian Education, but that morning I decided there were many opportunities for children's education other than at 9:30 a.m. on Sundays.

Take Back the Neighborhood
In my office there were two large windows. Each was about four feet wide and eight feet tall. I had a full view to the north and to the west. I was so immersed in finding the good in that project that I had failed to notice the drug commerce on my own. The police came one day and asked if they could film drug sales from the window of the church on the third floor. When I expressed surprise about the presence of drug sales, the officer stood at my desk and began pointing out the drug activity in the immediate area.

"Why don't you do something about that?" I asked.

"That is why we are here," he said, "but we need your help. Would you get the people in the community together and ask them what they would like to see changed about their neighborhood?"

116

The announcements went out. The first Saturday morning there were 20 people in the church fellowship hall. The following Saturday there were 35, then 55, then 75. The police attended each session and heard complaints and offered suggestions. I gave permission for the police to film using the large window on the third floor. I gave this permission without calling a Trustees' meeting or a meeting of the church Board.

In the midst of the filming, I began to fear for the church building and my own life. A grabber is not much protection if one messes with drug dealers.

It was then I remembered a story I heard from Bishop Leontine Kelly. Her father once pastored Mt. Zion Church and her brother was now an active member. She told of an experience when she was a child in another church in Cincinnati where her father was the pastor. The church had discovered an opening behind the furnace in the parsonage basement. They explored the opening and found it was a tunnel that went into the church basement. Slaves would go into the church, and when slave hunters went in after them, they had already gone through the tunnel and into and out of the parsonage as a part of the Underground Railroad.

When Bishop Kelly would tell the story, she would pause for a long moment and then say, "Can you imagine a church Board meeting or Trustee meeting taking a vote on building such a tunnel? That can only take place by people who had a vision of an injustice and a solution, and so they acted."

That day the police left, and I heard nothing more for three weeks. The community group continued to meet. Some were beginning to wonder if anything would change.

Then the call came from the police. "We will be there this afternoon."

I was in my office at 3:00. It appeared to be a normal day. I watched out the window. A U-haul truck pulled up. Not unusual for the neighborhood. The truck backed over the curb and the driver went to the back and opened the door. Out came thirty police officers with hoods over their heads. Quickly police cars and paddy wagons were all over the neighborhood. Television and news people filled the neighborhood. Twenty-two people were arrested.

The next Saturday 110 people were at the community gathering and, two weeks later, "Take Back the Neighborhood" was launched. The mayor and the city council members showed up with rakes and shovels. City trucks and crews went to work on the neighborhood. The local paper carried front-page stories of the neighborhood and the drug bust.

It was truly a community event to change the neighborhood.

We used one of the rooms of the church for a Children's Library. Rich and Jenny Housh, from the Lebanon Church, provided several thousand dollars to get the library operating. Many from Mt. Zion Church gave money and time. A person with experience in early childhood education from the neighborhood became the librarian. It was a wonderful sight to see many children from the neighborhood spending time in the Library.

I have mentioned before that the appointive system, with all its weaknesses, still takes one to places they never would have gone, to do things they never would have thought of, and to have experiences they never would have dreamed of.

Did I "hear" this call or "think" this call?

The question was irrelevant.

I was here, in the midst of God's land, with God's people, and I can say for sure that, each new day I was there, it was my calling.

Chapter 21

One particular time I strongly felt my call to Mt. Zion was when I visited a church member, Ernest Mills, at his home. While there, he went to the closet and, from high on the shelf, he took a box, opened it, and showed me a slave bill of sale for his great grandfather. Holding the tattered bill in my hand, knowing it was for the sale of a human being, moved me. Sitting in the presence of the grandchild of the one put on the auction block, I realized, once again, the great honor of being a United Methodist pastor.

If you truly open yourself up, ministry will take you places you never imagined.

Early on in my ministry, I had always tried to call on church members on or close to their birthday and ask questions about their journey. I made notes and tried to follow up on future birthdays.

I asked such questions as, "What is the earliest thing you can remember? What are three events that have had a great impact on your life? Give a sequence of your life from your birth to now. How long do you want to live? For what would you like to be remembered?'

There were other questions, but these were the essence of the birthday call. I stumbled onto this, and it became a meaningful part of ministry.

I had the honor and privilege of hearing so many beautiful, important stories. I discovered that each person on earth has a beautiful, important story.

The Power of Freedom
At the Norwood Church, Ray Brookbank was, for the most part, confined to a wheelchair. Almost daily he would scoot down the basement steps to a workshop. It was an easy task to secure a second wheelchair, so he would have one when he got down the steps scooting one by one on his behind.

A minister can quickly see a need and come up with a solution that delights the parishioners.

When I asked Ray Brookbank the three things that made a difference in his life, the first was when he got fired from Proctor and Gamble.

Ray said, "I realized I had limitations, and I would need to seek employment that would embrace those limitations. But soon it became a lifesaver for me as it forced me to come to terms with reality."

"Ray, how long do you want to live?" I asked him.

"I really do not know," he said, "but death is okay because I know that, in death, I will really be free. I want to be buried in a wooden casket with rope handles and I want those who carry me and bury me to know that they are setting me free."

Ray died some time later, and when I went to his funeral, the casket was metal with metal handles. I was prepared. I took long pieces of rope and tied them to the metal handles and then told of Ray's wishes.

At the graveside, Ray's daughter, his only child, said "When you put the rope handles on Daddy's casket, I wanted to stand and cheer. He told me the same thing, and I was sitting there thinking I had let him down. When you began tying on the rope handles I thought, "'Yes! That is what my Daddy wanted.'"

The Power of a Father's Love
One of the outstanding moments in Dave Shafer's life occurred at his high school graduation. For most of his life, he had never really felt connected with his father.

"He was there," Dave said, "but I did not really know if he knew I existed. As graduation approached I realized most of the boys would be wearing suits. I'd never had a suit, and I lay awake wondering how I could get by. What would happen if I showed up in my regular school outfit, and would they even let me in the graduation ceremony? The day before graduation my father said, 'Come on, Son.' He took me to a store and bought me my first suit. I will always remember the feeling of standing in that suit. My anxiety slipped away as I realized that, yes, my dad did know I existed."

When David died, I told that story at his funeral. His older son came up to me later and said, "I had never heard the graduation suit story and, to think, the minister was the one to share that magic moment with me."

Why the father had not told the story I do not know. Perhaps there was never a reason to share it, or perhaps he was never asked, but it surely was a story that was a rare privilege to hold and to share with his family after he died.

The Power of Memory
One morning I met Napoleon Helm for breakfast at Frisch's Restaurant in Cincinnati. I asked him those same questions. The earliest thing he said he could remember was his mother pulling him and his two brothers out of bed late at night and hiding down beside the bed.

The bright torch of the KKK lit up their home.

"Come out of the house, or we will come in and kill you!" the hooded man on the horse yelled.

Nap's Mother held him and his brothers close and said, "Shhhhhhhhhh!"

'We know you are in there!" the hooded men screamed. "Come out now! You do not belong here. We will get you! If not tonight, then sometime soon!"

"Shhhhhhhhh!" his Mother kept repeating.

The Klan vowed to be back, but that night they turned and rode away.

"That was over 70 years ago," Nap told me, "but sometimes, at night, I wake up, and I can hear their threats and almost see the bright torches."

Then he put his head on the table and wept.

Then he began singing, "Soon and very soon, we are going to see the King. Soon and very soon, we are going to see the King. Soon and very soon, we are going to see the King. Hallelujah! Hallelujah! We are going to see the King!"

The song had become familiar to me after I was at Mt. Zion for awhile. At the end of every funeral held at the church, the casket would be rolled slowly up the long center aisle. The family would follow and then, row by row, all those at the funeral. The whole time everyone was singing, "Soon and very soon, we are going to see the King."

Each time, I was moved deep in my soul when I led the casket and the people to the street outside the church.

One night late I received a call that Nap Helm was in the hospital and was having to be restrained. I went immediately and was stopped by a nurse outside his room.

"We had to restrain him, so you will find his feet and his hands are tied. We are afraid he will get out of bed and hurt himself. He has not been coherent all day."

"May I remove the restraints while I am in the room, if I stay right there?" I asked.

"You can try to keep him in bed, but there are no guarantees. He does not even know where he is."

When I walked in the room, Nap looked at me and said, "Reverend, I have needed you all day."

As I began untying the restraints he began singing another of his regular songs, "I woke up this morning with my mind, with my mind, stayed on Jesus."

I pulled up a chair beside his bed as he finished the song. "What is going on with you, Nap?" I asked.

"Been seeing the bright lights," he said, "and they say they are coming to get me, and I can't find my mother to take care of me. I don't know what to do."

And again he broke into song. "Soon and very soon, we are going to meet the King. Soon and very soon, we are going to meet the King! Soon and very soon, we are going to meet the King. Hallelujah! Hallelujah! We are going to meet the King!"

As he sang, I took his hand and carefully tied it to the side of the bed. And when each of the ties was secured, I prayed and left the room. In two days, I returned. Nap Helm's bed was empty. They said he was sent home, and on Sunday morning, he was in his usual place of worship.

The Power of Truth
Marian Spencer told me that, as a child, she stood on the front porch in Gallipolis, Ohio with her grandfather. The Klan was marching, white robes and torches and Marian said, "That night my grandfather said to me, 'Don't be afraid,' and right then he took the robes off several of the Klan and revealed who they were. He didn't literally take them off, but he told me about some of those who were hiding under them. He told me the robe was so people couldn't tell who they were."

Marian continued, "He took my hand and said 'See, that one in the middle of the front row. See, he is limping. That is the man who sells you penny candy across the street from your school.' That night my grandfather gave me a great gift. He literally took away the fear for a little girl of the KKK."

The Power of Risk Taking
I stood at the bedside of an older member of Mt. Zion. He was struggling with recovery from surgery. That night, as I sat by his bed, he told me of the Tuskegee Airmen. Black pilots were not permitted to fly with white pilots, so the Tuskegee Airmen were formed. They became great pilots.

One day Eleanor Roosevelt showed up and rode with one of the Tuskegee pilots. She went back to tell her husband, the President, that they were good, really good, pilots and he should put them into action immediately.

Roosevelt did, and the Tuskegee Airmen were instituted and went down in history.

The Power of Presence

When we were moving into the parsonage, I noticed the plaster was coming off one of the walls in the dining room. United Methodist pastors living in parsonages are often quick to call the Trustees and say, "Look here, what are you going to do about this?"

Don Spencer came by the parsonage, looked at the wall, and said, "Something needs to be done about that." He then said, "When Marian and I got married, we were lucky to find a decent place to live. Often housing was scarce for African-Americans. When we found a place we were so relieved that some of the things needing done to the house sometimes took a backseat to the joy of finding a place to live. When our first child was born, there were several hospitals, but Blacks could not get into them. The Salvation Army had a place where a Black couple could go to give birth to a child."

"If we are sometimes slow about getting things done, you just keep on us. We need to get that wall taken care of."

When Don left, Wende and I moved a secretary in front of the wall. It completely covered the plaster problem. The wall never crossed our minds after that.

The story Don told enhanced our understanding of what life was like, just a short time ago, for the members of my congregation.

One Sunday afternoon Don and Marian came over and sat on the front porch. During the worship service earlier that day, someone who was not supportive of my being there had spoken out in the worship service words of opposition and displeasure.

Don and Marian made no reference to what had happened. They simply came and said, "We wanted to sit with you for a while."

They did, and their unspoken message was clear. It was the kind of action that is at the heart of the faith. If a picture is worth a thousand words, then the words "we wanted to sit with you for awhile" just may be better than a thousand pictures.

I am aware that most of these stories give a positive spin to ministry. Perhaps you're wondering why I don't write more about the negative side, those things that cause clergy to want to give up and find a better place to spend their working life. The negative experiences were certainly present, and I would not want to leave the impression that my years were free of struggles. Indeed you have read many of them.

The reality is that all professions and jobs have those negative moments. The negative moments can be a part of the beautiful experience of a ministry, or they can become the lessons through which the life of a pastor is interpreted.

What I really believe is that any occupation, and especially the ministry, is a mindset. Decide it is a great privilege, and it will be. Decide it is a heavy load and filled with difficulties, then it will be.

In the context of a life filled with meaning, the difficult experiences become a part of the painting of the canvas of one's ministry.

As I sat and listened to story after beautiful story told by my dear parishioners, my mind often went back to the Mennonite evangelist's prayer that set my life on a course filled with meaning, all of which the pages of this book could not hold.

Grayson Atha

Chapter 22

"Grayson," said the voice on the end of the line. "The Bishop asked me to call you."

It was April 1994. The caller was Bob Woods, my district superintendent.

He continued. "She wants to know if you would be willing to make a move this year. There is a church with your name all over it."

I took this to mean there was a church out there that needed a pastor, and I had the gifts the Bishop and Cabinet felt the church needed.

"Well," I said, "where exactly is this appointment with my name written all over it?"

"Can't tell you," Bob shot back, "until you say whether or not you are willing to move."

"I'll talk with Wende," I told him. "I'll give you a call tomorrow."

The next day I called him to say we were agreeable to a move.

"Fantastic!" Bob said. "I've already got the introduction set up for this Wednesday. Will that work for you?"

"Now, Bob," I said, "how could you have the introduction set up for this Wednesday when you didn't even know if I would be willing to move?"

"Well that was easy," he said, "The Bishop said she was betting you were going to say 'yes' to being ready to move, but if you didn't, she was prepared to do some 'Bishoping' in order to persuade you, so I thought it best to line up the introduction."

I hung up the phone with that unique feeling in my heart. Every pastor who has taken a call like that from their district superintendent will understand. It's a mixture of hope, anticipation, a little bit of sadness, with just a touch of fear and trepidation mixed in.

And I admit to wondering, who exactly had written my name all over that church—God? Or the Bishop and the Cabinet?

Or perhaps both?

Starting Over Once Again

It was a hot day when we arrived in Columbus. The house we had rented a block from the church was not air-conditioned. It was a wonderful old house, built in the late 1800's.

There was sadness as we began to set up the new house, because Maggie, our cat, was left behind. A family in the Lebanon church gave Maggie to us. She hated moving vans. When we moved from Findlay to Cincinnati she got on a remote closet shelf and stayed there for four days. Wende was determined to make this move more comfortable for Maggie. We would empty a room, fill it with her favorite things, lock the door, and post a sign: *Do not enter.*

Halfway through the move, the door to that room was opened, and Maggie was gone. When everything was loaded and the van was leaving, concern built around Maggie. Several neighbors, carrying cans of tuna and calling Maggie's name, helped Wende search the neighborhood. After several hours, Wende reluctantly headed for Columbus, shedding tears all the way.

Since we had been living in a church parsonage in Cincinnati, and a new pastor had not yet moved in, Marcus and Holly, two of our children, decided to stay through the night. Food was put out and checks were made on a routine basis. They prowled the North Avondale area through the night looking for any signs of Maggie.

Around 10:00 p.m., we called from Columbus to ask the children if there had been any signs of Maggie. There had not.

128

About three days later, as Wende was unpacking, she saw out of the corner of her eye a small tail-like shadow pass by the doorway. Questioning whether she had really seen anything at all, she followed the shadow. Looking around the room, she finally saw the very end of Maggie's tail sticking out from underneath a bed. Shrieks of joy, and more tears, alerted me to the fact that Maggie had decided to join us after all.

We were puzzled though. We couldn't (and still can't) figure out how she had gotten herself there. She hated moving vans. Both of our cars were parked over a block from the house, and we knew she had not been in either of those.

Eight years later, at age 21, Maggie died. Tim Fiske built a small wooden box and, with the grandchildren, we held a service in the backyard on Neil Avenue. We do not know how animals' minds work, but perhaps, once they have a home, they will do whatever is necessary to keep that home.

Maggie died without ever telling us how she got to Columbus.

A New Chapter Begins
Our first Sunday at King Avenue was a hot summer day. Like our house, the church did not have air-conditioning. The choir, usually on summer break, had extended the year for my first Sunday.

When I walked into the sanctuary of this church built in 1920, I was awestruck. It is a magnificent place of worship. Just being with people in that space provides renewal.

Over 200 congregants were in worship, and the choir loft was full. Just before the sermon, the choir sang, "Mine Eyes Have Seen the Glory." The director of the choir was the husband of the organist. Jim and Jan Linker had been around King Avenue for many years. As Jim led the choir, I noticed tears flowing from his eyes.

A stunning moment I will never forget.

When I got up to preach, I asked about Nancy Greiner. I paused for a long moment because, in my heart, I was really hoping she would appear. I somehow knew I might need her here at King Avenue more so than any other appointment.

But then I continued:

In the absence of Nancy, I bring you her message. At first you will not like me, but hang in there, soon you will find I am okay.

One of the realities of the United Methodist ministry is that clergy do not decide where they are going, and churches do not decide whom they get. Since the service began, I have been looking out over the congregation to see what I got—and you all can look up here at me and see what you got.

I am glad to be your pastor. We are about to embark on a journey together. The church is a fascinating place to be and just a bit crazy. In the church each week the offering plates are passed, money is given, and magic happens. Money is turned into ministry—meeting human needs, loving children, providing this magnificent place for worship, and so much more.

The church is amazing. Where else would someone go to a store, buy ingredients for a cake, go home, spend time baking and icing it, take it to the church, and then buy it—or someone else's cake or pie—for $20, and not even fuss a bit?

I am well aware that being here is to continue in a line of persons who have been pastors of this church. I stand on the gifts of ministry of those both living and dead. Those who have gone before us have left this place for us, and we are privileged to carry on the great traditions handed to us.

Let us never forget that we gather today in the name of the God who has given life to all of us. If it were not for God, and the message God has sent into the world, we would not be here. God is the reason for our existence.

None of us know what the future holds. We know something of what we have been, but we do not know what we will become. We do know that, as we walk into the future, the same God who guided those of the past will, with a pillar of fire, make the way clear as we walk together. So we do not know what we will become, but we do know that God will be working in our midst.

Let us continue.

Is Everyone Truly Welcome?
The next day I received an unannounced visitor—Brad Colegate, a physician at The Ohio State University.

"What is your stand on gay people and the church?" he asked, once seated in my office.

"Well," I said, "*The United Methodist Book of Discipline* states that homosexual persons are persons of sacred worth and should be welcomed in all United Methodist churches, that the rights of homosexual persons should be respected, and they should be afforded a place in the full life of the church."

"What I really wanted to know is what *you* think about the matter," he said.

"Well," I replied, "I pretty much stand at the same place."

He breathed a sigh of relief.

"Well," he said, "the gay people in this church, we always try to figure out where the new pastor stands, and this time the group decided, 'Let's just ask,' and they designated me to be the one to ask. I am sure the group will be pleased with my report. The last minister helped us be a bit more courageous, so here I am."

He reached in his briefcase, pulled out a piece of paper, and handed it to me. "Since you believe gay people have a full place in the church, will you put this in the Sunday bulletin?"

It read: "The Christian Gays meet every third Sunday for lunch and Bible Study after church. If you want to join us, call the church office, give your name and number, and someone will call you."

"Why call the church office?" I asked. "Why not just announce where the meeting will be held?"

"Perhaps later," he replied, "but, right now, none of us are out."

Thus I discovered a screening process of who is safe and otherwise. Here was a church secretary in place helping to bring people together for a Bible Study without a formal church vote or Trustees approval. Fortunate is one to have a church secretary who has insight and compassion and is a bridge in times of transition.

"May I come to your Bible Study?" I asked.

"Oh, I will take that up with the group," Brad said. "They have to decide with whom they feel safe."

I got permission and went to a Bible Study. When I arrived at the house there were seven or eight people present. By the time we were eating, the group had grown to twenty. I discovered that over half of the group had stayed back in other parts of the house waiting to see what was going to happen when a preacher came to dinner. By the time of the discussion, everyone had joined in.

I told them my knowledge of the trials of homosexuality was limited, but I would be willing to learn about their battles if they would be willing to share them with me. I wanted to find out more about who they were as people, but would they be willing to let their defenses down?

Two weeks later I asked the leader where the next meeting would be held, because I wanted to attend. He said, "I have to ask to see if it is okay." I soon discovered that, for me and for them, the journey had begun, but it would be an interesting road we would travel together. Since I was the pastor of the church I wondered, too, about the church traveling that road with us.

And why would the road even be traveled anyway? There were many significant ministries already in place.

I thought of The King's Way Singers, a college-age group of singers filled with enthusiasm and committed to Christ. There was a "knock-down" Rummage Sale run by the United Methodist Women twice a year involving over one hundred people and providing close to $20,000 a year for mission projects. We had Disciple Bible Study Groups, a Stephen Ministry group, a growing awareness of ministry with children, a Christian Jazz Band, a music program most churches would envy, and a $300,000 budget to manage.

Would even modest attention to a new direction with one group put in jeopardy these good ministries already in place? I had been a United Methodist pastor for 30 years and I had a pretty good idea of how to survive, but is survival what ministry is about?

Thankfully there was time to deal with these questions and their answers.

Chapter 23

When we arrived at King Avenue, in the summer of 1994, there were those who volunteered to help us find our way, to get settled in, to feel comfortable.

Tom and Sandy Trinter were two of those people. One afternoon, they rented a small van and a guide and took us on a tour of Columbus and then to a wonderful restaurant for dinner. The Trinters were in worship every Sunday. They sat in the next to last row on the King Avenue side. Often, there were four generations of Trinters present.

I always looked forward to stopping by to see Sandy Trinter. She was a school principal. I know she had difficult, discouraging things to deal with every day. One of the reasons I liked to stop by is I always came away thinking that being a school principal was a life filled with meaning. When I would walk through the halls with her, children would run up to talk with her, and the little ones would hug her. When we sat together in her office, the stories of the school were touching. There were times when I would see her at church and I would say, "Tell me the story again of…" and then mention a story she had related.

Public schools in a city like Columbus often get a bad rap. People like to say, "I am moving out of Columbus to get a better education for my children." I wish they could experience the Sandy Trinters and the Sue Burts, and a host of others, who chose to experience teaching as a rare gift and privilege.

If I had to find a fault with public schools, it would be that they do not tell the stories of great things going on inside their walls. I have often thought, in retirement, I would like to become a storyteller for public schools. Poke around and find the Sandy Trinters, and then find a way to tell the whole world.

Warmly Welcomed

We also received a brief presentation from Jeff Wyckoff, a Five Star Chef at Macy's, on the restaurants to visit early on. There was no shortage of food dropped off at our home on Neil Avenue, and offers to help us settle were more than generous. The church had a beautiful reception on our first Sunday following the worship service. The church parlor was a sea of well-wishers and church members eager to bring us into the King Avenue fold. Most churches know how to welcome new pastors, and the personal touch at King Avenue was no exception.

Jim and Jan Linker invited Wende and me to a Chinese restaurant early in our time there. They were instrumental in the ongoing King's Way Singers, and their son was the director of this dynamic singing group.

The Linker's daughter Jenny had died several years earlier. It was a sudden death and a great shock to the whole congregation. Jenny was a vivacious college student at Otterbein, filled with love that spilled over into the hearts and minds of many others. She was musically talented and had a winning personality. A plaque with her name hangs in the sanctuary of King Avenue Church.

After dinner at the Chinese restaurant, Jan and Jim took Wende and me to their home and showed us Jenny's room. It remained much like it was when she died. We stood in the room together and talked for a long time about the church and Jenny and how they and others had put life together after her tragic death. They spoke especially of how faith in God and the church were crucial in the ongoing process of their healing.

Celebrating a Beautiful Couple

Every church needs a Carson and Helen Haney. Although they would be classified as senior citizens, both in their nineties, their presence was a dynamic force at King Avenue. Why they were loved so dearly has much to do with their friendliness—a kinds of friendliness that is not practiced or pretense.

Carson made it his business to greet everyone who came into the church. As he moved from place to place, he was usually humming a hymn or something else of a catchy nature. Carson didn't do this as a member of any committee or as an assigned greeter—he just naturally reached out to all those who came within his range. He even tried to seek out those who *hadn't* crossed his path.

The two of them were pure gold, and it was an honor to be their minister in my years there. Many people, when asked why they joined King Avenue, would reply it was the welcome of Carson and Helen. Their venue was the parlor and, from there, they served coffee and donuts before the 10:45 service.

Helen cut each doughnut into about five or six pieces. There was a school of thought at King Avenue that the donuts should be served whole. This school lovingly accused Helen of trying to save money on the donuts, to which Helen readily admits. The "non-cutters" on several occasions have attempted to change the way Helen serves donuts. They usually had some immediate success—but as soon as they let down their guard, thinking they have won the battle, the donuts again appear in bite-sized pieces.

It is interesting to note that, when The Morning Blend service began in 2001, the donuts served on the first Sunday were sliced "Helen-style." This has never been challenged, as far as I know.

Let the Little Children
On the occasion of their 50th wedding anniversary, I asked Carson and Helen if I could recognize them in the worship service. They agreed but requested it be done during the Children's Moments. They had no children of their own.

Children's Moments occurs each Sunday at some point during the worship service. A huge bouquet of helium-filled balloons is carried around the sanctuary and, as it passes by the children, they take their place behind the balloons. Sometimes there are fifty children or more. The crib room and nursery personnel all work together so the whole church can experience the children. Sometimes the littlest children come down in a big wagon or push cart.

Whenever a child is baptized, it happens during Children's Moments with the children and the congregation participating in the vows. Helen brings the water down to the front, and one of the children (sometimes a sibling of the baby) climbs a set of steps made especially for the purpose of helping them reach the baptismal font, and pours in the water. The new baby is held up high above the heads of the congregation, welcomed to this world, and offered as a sign from God that life is good and will continue. Then we all sing to the newly baptized one in our midst, "Child of Blessing, Child of Promise, baptized with the spirit's sign: with this water God has sealed you; unto love and grace divine."

There is no sight or sound sweeter than these children being serenaded by the people that have helped, and I truly believe will continue helping them, come to know and to love God.

Bible stories are sometimes told to the children, but there is not an attempt to convey a particular teaching or concept. We have skits and stories, dramas and prayer, but most of all, the time is designed to be special moments for children.

What Makes a Family?
It was in this setting that the Haneys agreed to have their 50th Anniversary recognized. Since this particular Children's Moment was to become a crucial moment in the life of the church, I here present it as it was recorded that November Sunday in 1994.

Grayson: Will the children please come at this time? (pause) I want to be able to see all of you. Would you come right out here a minute? Let me see. I want to look at everybody here. I want to tell you, if any of you have parents or anyone you know in the choir, feel free just to wave at them when you come down. Okay? We have a very special event this morning that I'd like for you to participate in. How many of you are in a family? (pause) Well, you know, do you know what a family is? What is a family?

Child: Yes.

Grayson: What is a family?

Child: It's some, it's a lot of people who live together, and the kids are someone that came out of someone.

Grayson: Okay! You ask a question, you get an answer. (laughter) Well, thank you very much. There are all kinds of families. There are sometimes, often, there's a man and woman and they have children and that is what you were talking about, weren't you? They have children, and that's a family.

Sometimes there's just a mother and children, and that makes a family. And sometimes there's just a father and children and that makes a family. Sometimes there are two men, sometimes there are two women, sometimes there's a man and a woman who live together for a long time and then one of them dies and they're just a family of one then. And sometimes there's a father and mother who adopt a child, and they're a family.

So, there are many different kinds of families in our world, but there is something that is the same about every family. Do you know what that is? (pause) They are loved and cared for at King Avenue Church. Every family has a place and is loved and cared for at King Avenue Church, because we are one big family together.

And I'd like to ask Carson and Helen Haney to come up here for a minute. I want you children, you have seen them and you know them, but I want you to see them right now on this special day for them. They are coming right down this aisle here.

These are one of the special families in our church and they have been married today for fifty years. They were married in this church. Isn't that something?

They're one of the families, and they are a part of us and they are loved and cared for, and we want to thank you for being around here for so long and for being one of our special families.

And children, I would like for you to stand up here and if you would stand in a line on either side of the Haneys—would one of you take their hand then join hands right across the front here? Will you do that? (Whispered: Come up further. Come on up.) Join hands with them.

And let's make this all around the sanctuary. Let's all stand and join hands and join together as we are one family and let's sing together. (Everyone singing the following:)

> *Blest be the tie that binds our hearts in Christian love.*
> *The fellowship of kindred minds is like to that above.*
> *We share each other's woes, our mutual burdens bear,*
> *and often for each other flows the sympathizing tear.*

Grayson: O, God, thank you for all of the families of this congregation. We pray that you will be with them, uphold them, guide and direct them. Thank you for the Haneys and we pray that you will give them strength and rest and health and wisdom that they may follow you all the days of their lives. In Christ's name. Amen.

Thank you children very much.

That evening, my phone rang. It was Bob Heber, the Staff Parish Chairperson. He got straight to the point.

"Reverend Atha," he said, "I think you have just committed ministerial suicide."

Chapter 24

A lump formed in my throat, and my stomach twisted in a knot. Ministerial suicide. What had I done?

Bob Heber had been a part of the church for over forty years. He would be what some call an "old-timer.'"

"I am calling a special meeting of the Staff Parish Relations Committee for tomorrow evening," he said. "Can you be there?"

"I never miss a special meeting," I replied, "but what is going on?"

I think, if I would have had to guess at that point, I could have predicted as a few hints had been dropped since the service. In the United Methodist Church, news spreads fairly quickly by word of mouth. I knew this, but it didn't lessen the sense of anxiety that washed over me when I got the call.

The words *ministerial suicide* kept reverberating in my head along with visions of the down payment Wende and I had just made to purchase the house we had been renting on Neil Avenue. We had never owned a house before. How would we sell so quickly? To what church would I be reappointed, or would I even receive another appointment?

And, if this was all such a shock to me, why had I brought the issue forth in the first place?

"Some folks are upset about the Children's Moments," Bob said. "I have received eighteen calls, and I want to get the Committee together and talk about it."

Eighteen calls. Clearly the rush of blood through my beating heart was a sound only I could hear. He did not seem to be aware of it.

The Meeting

There were eleven persons on the Staff Parish Relations Committee. The group met monthly. Usually, at the regular meeting, there would be at least five present, sometimes six or even eight. On this night all eleven were present sitting on the couches and in the over-stuffed chairs in the East Parlor.

Not one person was late.

Bob Heber opened the meeting with prayer and then proceeded to suggest a format for the meeting. He would report on the eighteen calls and then go around the room to receive comments from the members of the Committee. Everyone present agreed to this format.

Then an amazing thing happened. In all my years as a pastor I had never experienced this before. Often a committee member will say, "I received a phone call" or "a party called me." Bob Heber had his list, said each person's name, and reported the essence of the conversation.

He had then taken it a step further. Before the meeting, he had called each person back and asked, "What do you want the Committee to do?" Bob reported that there were few suggestions or solutions.

When Mr. Heber had completed reporting on each of the eighteen persons he had received calls from, he then asked committee members to give input.

I Wasn't Prepared for This

Brad Colegate went first. He told about going to a small community United Methodist Church when he was a child. At about twelve, he began to notice he was different. He was not as interested in boy-girl relationships as others in his church youth group and felt he was more attracted to boys than girls. This worried Brad greatly. What was happening? There was really no one to talk to—not his teacher, not his minister, not his parents—and, of course, if he tried to check out any books from the school library, he would have to explain.

So Brad prayed God would change him. Change his thoughts and desires. Here was a thirteen-year-old boy trying to find his way, and

142

there was no open door. Brad prayed and prayed, and it did not help. The feelings and desire were still there, and the feelings and desires expressed from his peers did not match his own.

"So, I quit going to church," Brad said. "I carved out a little life of my own, not talking to anyone about it and, when I got to college and then medical school, I simply felt safer but still did not go to church. Then someone invited me to King Avenue. I had sometimes wanted to get back to church, so I accepted their invitation. I liked what I found. I sang in the choir; I helped with the rummage sale; I baked things for the bake sale. I made a pledge to the church every year. I have been through Disciple Bible Study and Stephen's Ministry. I listen to people talk about their families and their lives, but I never talk about myself, and no one really asks me."

"I think, for me and some of the rest of us, we need to know, are we welcome only if we keep quiet, or is there a place for us the way we are?"

Next a man on the couch jumped out of turn and said, "We have a son who is gay."

Another spoke up and said, "I have a brother who is gay."

Another member of the committee said, with tears in his eyes, "We had a nephew who committed suicide. He was just a teenager. We were never sure, but some members of the family believed he was struggling with homosexuality."

The meeting lasted over two hours and, by the end of the meeting, there were many tears, a lot of hugging, and it seemed to me the storm had passed. I did not realize that the storm was not passing, rather the storm clouds were just gathering. The road, if it were to be traveled, would be long and treacherous with casualties, still unforeseen, along the way.

As I was leaving the meeting, I stopped Brad Colegate to tell him what a wonderful statement he had made.

"How many times have you done that speech before?" I asked.

"Never," he said. "And I was nervous. Just before I left work to come here, I asked the person who works in the office beside me if he had a few minutes so I could practice a speech on him.

"When I finished, he said, 'Brad, I did not know that, and I have worked with you for seven years. It is a magnificent speech—give it just like you gave it to me.'"

A Place to Call Home

As I sit here, with pen in hand, I realize I really needed to believe the storm was passing and that suddenly everything would be all right. I really needed to believe my experimentation with ministerial suicide was brief and had come to an end.

But the storm that was forming was far bigger than even what I had put in motion, or could have predicted was coming. Already we were reaping the rewards of facing some of the unspoken words in our midst and some of our closed doors to those very people we professed to love and bring closer to God.

Something happened that night in the parlor that had never happened quite this way in the 110-year history of the church. The church had a strong foundation. The people of King Avenue in the past had welcomed the stranger, the outcast. Things had happened in the community because King Avenue Church was there.

But, that night, the words were spoken, and the questions were asked. We questioned our own path. The subject of homosexuality was laid on the table, out in the open, to be talked about, asked about, and we wondered, if not aloud, then to ourselves, "Are people who are gay or lesbian welcome in our midst?"

A decision was made that night that "Yes we can talk about this—it is okay to say the words, to acknowledge those among us who are gay or lesbian."

How this would happen, no one knew.

That was the night we began the journey that would say to all people, "Our hearts, our minds, our doors are open. Here is a place where you will be loved and accepted."

That was the night a 13-year-old found a place he could call home.

Grayson Atha

Chapter 25

Whenever there is an issue in the church—whether a building program, change of pastors, a space issue, or financial crisis—there are always two entities at work. First, there is the official body, the board, and committees assigned to deal with the matter. Then there are the conversations going on around the church about the issue.

Sometimes this is quite helpful, but often discussion takes place in an atmosphere where participants have limited knowledge of the issue. The information is not secret or unavailable but often folks, especially church folks, do not feel they need the facts to weigh in on a matter.

That is one of the great things about a church—everyone can hold an opinion and, in such discussions, most everyone can be the boss.

During King Avenue's time of "opening our doors," there were many discussions among members of the church. We also discovered there were many discussions and attempts to inform the people of King Avenue about what they should think and why. It seems that, whenever there is an issue in our society or the church that causes people to choose sides, both sides are often uncomfortable with the presence of the other side.

The Struggle for Unity
It is somewhat like the church whose congregation had two points of view on applause. Some believed clapping in church was appropriate and helpful, completely in order. Others felt clapping was inappropriate in the church setting.

The pastor thought he had the perfect solution. Those who wanted to clap should clap. Those who did not should not clap. On the surface it seemed like a reasonable solution. What the pastor failed to realize was that, while the clappers were clapping, they would notice the non-clappers and immediately feel out of place clapping. At the same time, the non-clappers, seeing the clappers clap, wondered if perhaps they should be clapping after all.

It is difficult for one group to hold two different opinions precisely because of the lack of certainty in all of us. We are more comfortable when everyone thinks and acts like us.

King Avenue was no different. After the infamous Children's Moment, the Staff Parish Relations Committee met monthly. The issue of homosexuality and King Avenue was almost always a topic for discussion. Committee members received many phone calls trying to get each member to embrace their point of view. This lobbying was not limited to the telephone; it happened at church meetings, on the street, in restaurants, at sporting events, in the aisles of grocery stores, and especially in and around the milling area before and after worship.

The Staff Parish Relations Committee chairperson who succeeded Bob Heber told me he sometimes needed to come late to worship, sit in the back, and leave on the last hymn just to avoid the intense conversation on Sunday morning.

The reality is that both sides had a high interest in the church and its future. Many had given years of service and countless hours toward the mission of King Avenue. Relatives, family, and friends had helped make the church what it was and were determined to keep it within the pattern they felt it was molded.

And then there were those who believed the church was headed in the wrong direction, and they felt a great burden to say the right things, talk to the right people, and formulate arguments in such a way that what they presented as reason would prevail.

I write this here because, if you are a part of another church trying to "open your doors," you can absolutely count on this as a challenge.

The SPRC would spend one to two hours coming to an agreement such as: "The words *gay* and *lesbian* are appropriate to use from the pulpit in the proper context." Once the meeting was over, and the word began to get out, the committee members were bombarded as to why this agreed-upon decision was an extremely bad idea.

Reasons such as "using the words will give the wrong idea to visitors," or "children will think we are promoting homosexuality" or "young people who sing in King's Way Singers will have parents visiting and will pull their children out of King Avenue" or "people who have given generously to the church will be offended and quit giving" or "using those words put us in conflict with *The Book of Discipline of the United Methodist Church*" or "using those words is a violation of biblical teaching."

So the committee members would leave meetings with a sense of agreement, but the phone calls and conversations, with an appeal to friendship and the past and future of the church, would result in much second-guessing of their own positions. This was emotionally exhausting for the members of the committee.

Of course the resources on this subject seem to be endless—books, magazines, videos, sermons, pamphlets, and opinions of friends. The reality is that there is a lot of material on both sides of the issue, but there is a tendency to gather only the information favorable to one's position. Once bolstered with written expertise, many people proceeded directly to the nearest SPRC member to share with them their compelling information.

And there is another dynamic—the threats of some church members that, "if it does not change, we are going to leave." This adds a whole new element, because relationships have been established over the years, emotional ties have been made, weddings and baptisms celebrated. With the intertwining of relationships, we can begin to understand how no single issue is cut and dry.

A Balancing Act
In the midst of monthly meetings, I was a part of the interview process for the Conference Board of Ministry. I was the leader of a team of five who had the responsibility to interview six persons. I apologized to the group that I could not be present for an upcoming interview that conflicted with a SPRC meeting. Since I was 20% of the interview

team they naturally inquired as to why I would be absent. I told them a little about the issues we were working on, and suddenly while I was talking with them, it became clear what was happening at King Avenue.

I compared the situation at the church to moving an extension ladder when painting or working on a house. One can move the extension ladder in an upright position and then, while keeping it balanced, the ladder can be moved sideways. However, if the balance of power of the ladder shifts, and the ladder heads toward you there is a point of no return, and one had better get out of the way or there is a distinct possibility of being crushed by the ladder.

It was this delicate balance that I worked on day in and day out. Maintaining the balance consisted of phrases such as:

I understand your concern.

No, we surely would not want to turn people away.
Yes, the King's Way Singers are crucial to ministry here at King Avenue, and we don't intend to try to isolate them or their families.

We would not want to lose any families at all.

Yes, the children are very important to our ministry here.

You are right; if several people quit giving, it would present a hardship for the church.

Well, the reality is I do not talk about homosexuality all the time but, for those who do not want to hear those words at all, even one time seems like all the time.

I am called to minister to the whole congregation, not just those who are uncomfortable with the subject of homosexuality.

I know this is a long-standing belief, but God calls us in every generation to listen to what God may be saying to us now.

You can see these are all valid concerns that call for thoughtful answers. It is also apparent that, if the wrong answer is given, it could cause the ladder to fall from its delicate balance.

Listening to Concerns

There is another issue that has a profound impact if a church is moving toward inclusiveness. This issue is probably the most powerful and, if not dealt with, there is little possibility of moving forward.

I will illustrate this point by relating the conversation of three people who made appointments to come and talk about the direction of the church.

The first gentleman was very active in church finances. He had moved our church to a sound financial footing and had also made provisions for money to be left to King Avenue upon his death in a revocable Trust.

His first question to me was, "Do you plan to continue to push the homosexuality thing?"

I responded, first off, with a sincere thank you to him for approaching me directly. I explained that often people have an opinion but will not share it directly with the pastor. I told him that, when I first came to King Avenue, I discovered a group of gay persons who were no longer content to remain silent. They wanted to know if they had a full place in the church as gay persons, or were they welcome only if they kept quiet? I shared with him that I was simply attempting to assist them in finding their way.

He responded by stating that, before I came to King Avenue, that "group" was pretty well accepted. No one tried to run them off. They were participants in the full life of the church. But what he felt had changed was the constant talk about it. He emphatically stated that he and his family would be leaving the church if the conversation about gay people did not stop.

With sadness I explained to him that I felt there would be an empty place in the life of King Avenue without him. He had been an important part of the church for a long time, and I reminded him he was loved and appreciated by the people here. I clarified that I thought we could not move forward if we could not talk about it. I asked him, "If the church loves gays and provides a place for them here, then why can't we take the next step and talk about it?"

He finished by saying that talking about it was just going too far. He wanted to let me know they would indeed be looking for another church.

I had recently done the funeral for a member of his family, and we had shared many long talks. I felt comfortable offering a prayer with him before he left the office that day.

Six months later they transferred to another United Methodist Church.

Chapter 26

It's hard to describe the feelings of profound loss and sadness that come from conversations like this. And, of course, it always led me to a re-examination of whether "opening" the doors was the right thing to do. And was there a way to do it that would not isolate part of our King Avenue family?

I don't know that a day ever went by during this process that I did not ask myself those questions in order to try to find a way to "maintain the balance."

More Choose to Leave
The second person had held a volunteer position in the church for 25 years. He had also chaired the Administrative Council for the past eight years. His primary question to me was, "Do you foresee a time in the future that the whole subject of homosexuality will be dropped here at King Avenue?"

Again, I first of all thanked him for coming to me. I then explained that the gay persons of this congregation are experiencing a great relief because we are talking about it. Many of them, I told him, cannot talk about it at work. Some can't even tell their families or relatives, nor can they talk about it in social settings. I told him I was afraid that once this congregation has said, "We welcome you and we want you to tell us about yourself; what is life like for you?" that it would be hard to retract that sign of inclusiveness and freedom and return to a more closed environment.

He responded by stating he did not want there to be any surprises if we kept talking about homosexuality. One day, he told me, when I looked into the congregation on Sunday morning, he and his family would no longer be present.

"I am deeply sorry to hear you say that," I told him. "You have been an important part of this congregation for many years, and I wish there was some way to fix it so that it would be okay for everyone."

"Well," he stated, "it was fixed, but now it is broken. We have always welcomed gay persons here. They have been ushers, sung in the choir, have been on boards and committees of the church, but now, for some reason or other, some are trying to say that all along they were not welcomed and, unless we talk openly about them, they do not feel welcome. Didn't all those years count for something?"

I explained that, yes, they did count. The church did make a place for gay persons, and it was a wonderful beginning, but the gay persons have told us there is more needed than a passive acceptance. They feel that, if the words are off limits, then the acceptance is conditional.

Three months later he resigned both positions and left.

The third person was a key member of the staff who had been active in the church for 30 years. She was beloved by most in the church. Her musical talents are exceeded by only a few in the Columbus community.

The meeting began with her asking me when my homosexuality project would be coming to an end. "How much longer do you intend to pursue this?" she asked. "Are your goals about met, or are you going to pursue it until the church is completely destroyed?"

I explained to her that, whether she represented herself or others, I appreciated her caring enough about King Avenue and her church family to come and have this conversation with me. I emphasized to her the great appreciation I held for her and her musical talents, abilities, and gifts she brought to this church and told her how important it was to me that we resolve her concerns.

She stated that some of her very closest friends are gay as well as students of hers, and she emphasized that she had nothing against gay people. But she shared that she was certain, if we kept moving in the direction we were headed, the church would be destroyed. So she asked again how long I would be carrying out this project.

I clarified to her that this was not my project. I emphasized that I understood her concerns but explained that, before I came to King Avenue, there were gay persons here. These gay persons sang in the choir, ushered, were involved in Bible Study, tithing, Children's Ministry, etc.

"It seems you are saying that, before you came here, Pastor, we had it all! What happened?'"

"I guess what happened was my coming here coincided with the gay persons in this congregation being no longer willing to be kept silent. Gay people in society are told something is the matter with them; that they need to be fixed. So, the church contributes to this understanding by refusing to recognize them as gay persons. When I arrived, the gay persons here were ready to test the congregation to see if the church had a place for them as gay persons who sing, tithe, study the Bible, etc. or must they continue to hide their sexual orientation in order to have a place at the King Avenue table?"

She responded by saying she did not know about all of that. But she did know she did not hear those sentiments from the gays in this congregation, and surely not from the gay people she counted as her best friends. But she stated she did know, if I kept pushing this gay agenda of mine, this church would be destroyed, and she hoped I would get this out of my system before it was too late.

I explained to her that I never anticipated presiding over the destruction of a church when I became a minister. However, I learned early on that faithfulness to God is the ultimate goal of a pastor.

"Do you wonder if I have doubts about how all this will come out?" I asked her. "Yes, I do. However, if I should decide to make decisions based on the voices around me, then I have this haunting feeling I will have missed God's call on my life."

Shortly after our conversation she resigned the music position, saying she wanted to spend more time traveling with her husband.

Silence Speaks Loudly

So, silence is the main deterrent to an inclusive church. One might look at the above encounters and conclude that none of these conversations were examples of silence, but that is precisely the reason progress is so slow, that breakthroughs are so difficult to achieve. Sometimes silence is not golden; sometimes silence can be subtle, devastating, debilitating, stifling.

A pastor in a large United Methodist Church recently told me there was no problem with gay people in his church. Gay people attended the church and no one complained. He felt they were fully welcomed.

"In what ways do you talk about it?" I asked.

"Oh, we never talk about it," he said. "There is no reason to. No one really cares."

"Well, if you ever decide to talk about it, let me know," I told him. "The peace will end, and the time of adjustment will begin."

What is this anyway about the silence? There is something about us as human beings that, if we do not talk about something, then in our minds it is really not there. Words release the mind to reality.

Human beings have always had an uncanny way of ignoring what they do not want to face up to. There can be an alcoholic in the family, and the family can act like there is no issue. A marriage can be in serious trouble but, unless someone calls it by name, no resolution is possible.

And a church can have gay people in their congregation and yet live like they really are not there. They can be recognized but not seen. They can be accepted but not included. They can be welcomed but not embraced.

The issue of recognizing gay people at King Avenue became an ongoing issue. "They know they are welcome; why do we need to say it?"

What Does it Mean to be Welcome?
Gay people in the congregation offered two compelling reasons.

First, gay people often come looking for a church. Perhaps they went as a child and then found they were unwelcome. They may have a longing to get back to church, but the painful rejection of earlier years keeps them away.

Now, if they should come to King Avenue or any other church some Sunday, it is absolutely essential they hear a word of welcome. Every Sunday we make it a point to send a signal to any new person. There are many ways to say the words that, for the most part, would go unnoticed except for gay persons, such as:

There will be a couples' gathering next Friday. Bring your spouses, your partner, or significant other. Singles are also welcome.

Today we want to recognize all those who have been married or in a partner relationship for 10 years or longer. If this is you, please stand.

The Christian Gay, Lesbian, and Friends will have a "Meet and Greet" following the worship service.

It sounds very simple but, believe me, that's all it takes. Put it in, and you have welcomed all. Leave it out and uncertainty abounds.

The second thing is that it gets the church familiar with the language. You may not believe this, but some people have difficulty saying gay or lesbian, homosexual, bisexual or transgendered. These are real words that describe people in our society. They are not dirty words, obscene words. They are words like baby, teacher, doctor, and banker.

If it is difficult for us to say these words, it will be difficult for us to welcome everyone.

We have a time in our worship service for a witness. People talk about their personal faith. It is not unusual for a gay person to relate how they left the church when they discovered they were gay. They may end up by saying someone invited them to King Avenue and, when they entered the church, they felt they had come home. It is not unusual, as they leave the podium, for the congregation to clap, often enthusiastically, sometimes standing.

After one of these witnesses, an 85-year-old man came in my office and said, "Reverend, I just don't get it. Heterosexual people do not get up and say they are heterosexual. Why do gay people need to say they are gay? Who cares?"

I paused for a long time. Then I carefully answered. "Some people who stand in that pulpit are not able to say that to anyone else. They must keep quiet about it. Sometimes they can't even talk with their own family. But think what it means to them to stand before the church family and say 'I am gay, and I found Jesus again in this place,' and then hear people clap for them."

The elderly gentleman looked at me and said, "Reverend, you can stop right there. I get it!"

The Church Reaches a Verdict
When I arrived at King Avenue, I was 59 years old. I followed a young suave pastor. He and his wife both owned motorcycles. He had served King Avenue seven years and, during that time, the attendance had gone over the 300 mark several times. He had been instrumental in helping bring some gay people together.

In Disciple Bible Study, which he led, several gay persons came out and it was a very positive experience. It was during the seven years that Stan Ling was the pastor that gay people began to dream and touch the edges of what a church might be where they could freely live and move as gay children of God.

The first year I was at King Avenue the average worship attendance was 278. As people began to leave, and some others dropped off in their attendance, the average after three years was down to 248.

About this time a trial was held in Cincinnati. A former parishioner had brought a civil suit against me. The suit dragged on for four years. At the same time, I was trying to keep the ladder from falling over at King Avenue. Regularly, I had to go to Cincinnati for depositions and turn over phone records, letters, notes, and date books. Of course, information about the suit fell into the hands of some of those who were unhappy with my ministry at King Avenue. They found this to be further "proof" of my inability to lead a congregation.

The suit was brought by a gentleman with a history of suing companies and individuals for various reasons. He often received small settlements along the way that encouraged further endeavors. When the matter finally came to trial it lasted for seven days and, when the jury began deliberating, it took them ten minutes to determine there was no basis for the suit.

Meanwhile, there was mounting concern at King Avenue about the future of ministry in that setting. The time of year when each church was asked whether or not they would like the pastor to return for another year was upon us. This particular meeting was held in the latter part of 1997. The interest level was still high so that Staff Parish attendance was regularly running close to 11 people at each meeting.

These meetings were taking place all across the West Ohio Conference, and the general procedure includes discussion of any issue that needs to be covered. The pastor then leaves the room while further discussion and a vote takes place, determining the fate of the pastor (and the church).

Prior to the meeting, three people had given letters to each of the Staff Parish members outlining why it was important to have a change of pastors. One of the letters came from the staff member who had resigned to spend more time with her family. Now, in her letter, she apologized for not being truthful before with the committee. She related that the real reason she resigned was because she could not serve on a staff with a pastor who was not telling the congregation the truth about homosexuality.

I knew these three letters were all quite poignant about why there should be a change of pastors.

Before I left the meeting, I shared with the group that I was aware there had been considerable turmoil and that no doubt, with hindsight, there were probably ways I could have maintained "the balance" more effectively. But I felt, overall, the church was moving in a good direction.

However, if they felt it would be best to have a new minister, I would understand their decision. In 40 years of ministry, I had never been asked to leave a church before but others had, and I was sure it would work out.

I also asked that they recommend a Homosexuality Study Committee. I told them I was a lightning rod for this issue, and it was not about me, but the church and the direction it would take in the future. What the church does about gay persons is a decision the whole church must make. Ideally, the study committee would consist of 20 people, from a cross-section of the church, to be nominated by the Nominating Committee. This Committee would make recommendations to the Administrative Council on how the church would relate to gays and the issue of homosexuality.

These eleven people were thoughtful people. All of them cared deeply for the church. Many had roots that ran deep in the life of the church. Whatever decisions were to be made by these people would be made out of a love for the church and a deep concern for the future.

That night they voted unanimously in favor of a Homosexuality Study Committee.

And they voted six to five for me to leave the church.

Chapter 27

Churches are wonderful miracles. Churches deal with the mysteries of God using, as a main source, a book (The Bible) that was written over 2,000 years ago, using for a model a person (Jesus) who walked this earth 2,000 years ago and had a ministry that lasted about 3 years until his death at 33. Word spread that he rose from the dead and appeared to many people, but soon he was gone again, and no one has seen him since, although millions claim to talk with him daily.

Give that scenario to most anyone, changing the circumstances ever so slightly, and many would tell you that story does not have a chance of forming a movement.

In Praise of King Avenue Church

King Avenue is just one example as to how that story still lives. Based around the story, King Avenue Church has two services each Sunday, and people keep coming week after week because of a deep belief in the ways and teachings of Jesus Christ. They give money, cook meals, buy flowers, sing in choirs, participate in Disciple Bible Studies, go on Walks to Emmaus, lead A.W.E. experiences, teach Sunday School, sort rummage, and work at New Life.

The actions are endless.

And so the question: if King Avenue Church, and a multitude of other churches, follow Christ, why do so many tensions exist in these churches? Why do church people fuss and complain? Why do some break off and start new churches? Why do some become disgruntled and stop going to church?

And, based on Jesus' teachings of love and forgiveness, why do so many churches think, if they have a change of pastors, or change of service time, or change of carpet color or a merger or consolidation, that everything will be okay?

After considering all of the above, and after 47 years as a pastor, I really believe the fussing and complaining often represents disappointment in our own lives, and laying this disappointment at the door of the church becomes a convenience.

When I was asked to leave King Avenue in 1997, it was decided by a group of people who wanted the very best for the church then and in the future. They did not have to look far to see signs of a church going downhill. In recent years, during the pastorate of Stan Ling, attendance had averaged over 320 for a couple of years. Now it was hovering around 250. People had left the church, and more were threatening to do so. The church was struggling financially and, with all of this and more, why would it not be an obvious conclusion for the good of the church to have a change of pastors? I am absolutely sure no one acted out of spite or wrong motive. They were concerned for the future of the church with which they had been entrusted, and changing pastors seemed a reasonable approach.

The second question the Staff Parish Relations Committee dealt with that night was to establish a Homosexuality Study Committee. So a "yes" to that became easy as it proved that the requested pastoral change was not over the issue of homosexuality. The request for this study was proof of a genuine desire to identify the future of King Avenue and its stance on homosexuality.

Going Down Without a Fight?
Twenty-four hours after the decision was made, the chairperson of the Staff Parish Relations Committee informed me of the request for a change of pastors. I swallowed hard. It was not a surprise to me but, when one actually hears the words, the reality begins to take hold.

"What did they decide about the Homosexuality Study Committee?" I asked.

"They voted to move ahead with that," he responded.

I went home and informed the family we would be moving in June. I was not prepared for the reaction I received.

162

Outrage. And the most pronounced determination I have ever experienced from them in all my years of ministry.

"If you do not stand up for yourself and the future of King Avenue," they cried, "then you have lost your desire to even be in ministry!"

"Look," I said, "we will go quietly. I have seen churches in turmoil, and I have seen church fights, and I will be no part of that."

I related to them the story of my father when his neighbor asked him to go half and half on a fence. My father's reply was "Only if you decide where the property line is and decide what kind of fence would be best. Get it put up, then I will pay half."

My father added, "I have seen too many fights over property lines, and I will be no part of that."

My father's philosophy had become part of the fabric of my life.

"It is time you move beyond your father's philosophy," one of my children said firmly. "We loved him too, but he did not understand that good controversy worked out can make good neighbors, even better than the passive approach."

I could tell my family felt very strongly about this, and I made it a point to listen.

"Besides," this adult child continued, "this is not about property lines. This is not just about you and your future; it is about more than that. It is about a whole group of people in that church and, if you walk out of here quietly, you let all of them down. Now is their moment. Are you going to let them down?"

"What you say sounds good," I replied, "but it is obvious things are going downhill. People are leaving. Some are withholding their money. Do you want me to preside over a losing battle?"

"Wait a minute," one of them replied, "when Jesus was dying on the cross, everyone took off except the women. Did Jesus say, 'Well this is a losing battle, I can see that,' and give up? No. You do not know where this is going to go. You know you have told us often about how, in life, sometimes things have to get worse before they begin to get better. Well, right now for King Avenue, it appears things have gotten worse. How can you walk out of here with the knowledge that you may be standing on the edge of things beginning to turn around?"

Just then the phone rang. Wende answered it. I heard her say, "I do not think he wants anyone writing letters to anyone, but let me put him on the phone."

I soon discovered that word had gotten out on the decision to let me go. The decisions of Staff Parish Relations Committees are to be confidential and not revealed by the Committee as they are only advisory to the District Superintendent and the Bishop.

"Who do we send the letter to?" the caller asked after identifying herself.

"I really don't want anyone writing letters," I replied.

Marcus, Angie, and Holly came in the room to listen to the conversation and began motioning wildly at me to change its course. They could have just as easily been 8, 10, and 13 again, trying to motion to me that they were going to friends' houses for dinner. The emotion was as intense—but for different reasons this time. They were instead 30, 32, and 35 and trying to signal to me that I should allow the caller to write a letter, that I was out of my mind to stop the swell of support about to rise up on my behalf.

After saying goodbye to the caller, one of them asked, "Why do you think you have to run people's lives? Tell them what they can and cannot do! This is their church, too. This is bigger than you. You cannot contain this with your grandiose idea of how everybody should get along. Now, call them back and tell them you changed your mind."

I did as I was told, not because I necessarily agreed with what they said, but because I felt a trust in their wisdom I could not yet understand. I had never experienced my children this determined, and there were small hints within me that maybe they had a point.

I dialed the caller back and simply said, "You write to the District Superintendent and copy the Staff Parish Relations Chairperson and Bishop."

The next time the Staff Parish Relations Committee met, the chairperson walked in with a thick file of letters and began passing them around to the Committee members. There were letters of support for the Committee's decision and letters opposed. When they came to me, I passed them on without reading them.

A week later I went to the district superintendent's office and asked to see my file. I read for a long time and learned a lot about myself, and some of the people of King Avenue.

Two weeks later, the Bishop sent two district superintendents to meet with the Staff Parish Relations Committee. I was not invited to attend, and I received no report.

This was a time of great conflict because, while I was concerned about my own future, I had to put that aside. The decision that was made to formulate the study committee was a great silver lining to my own personal crisis of rejection by a church.

I had always preached that a church is bigger than a pastor, and the mission of a church is about its people, not the person up in front of them every Sunday morning. I had said that congregations are not led but guided. If I really believed that, then I had to look at this situation from the context of the people in this church who came before me and would be here long after I was gone.

The Committee is Finally Formed
In fact, there were days when I was focused more on the excitement of the permission to put the committee together than I was on my own struggle. So I did act rather quickly to call together the Nominating Committee to begin the process of nominating 20 people from a cross-section of the church to form The Homosexuality Study Committee.

The Nominating Committee decided trust was essential. The Homosexuality Study Committee must be made up of people who were respected and trusted so that, when their report was made, it would have the greatest possibility of careful consideration.

Each member of the Administrative Council and Nominating Committee was asked to list the five people they trusted most in the church. Then the Nominating Committee took their lists, compiled them into one list, and had the Administrative Council members check the ten people in which they had the highest level of trust.

From that list, the Nominating Committee selected twenty people: three college students, five long-time members, four parents, and four people who were also gay. There were two lawyers, a physician, three educators, a judge, and a scientist. Two people were in their eighties. The selected 20 were approved by the Administrative Council and they began their work.

King Avenue UM Church had its beginning in December 1888. The church was started to accommodate folks who lived in the neighborhood. There were many beautiful homes in the immediate vicinity, but that began to change when the larger homes were made into apartments and rooms for students. The Ohio State University is immediately to the north of the church. The church served many students, some in the neighborhood, but many came from the suburbs. However, they were folks who had lived in the neighborhood or had been involved with The University.

The Preface of the Homosexuality Study Committee Report to the congregation contains this paragraph:

In June 1994, Bishop Judith Craig appointed Grayson Atha as Senior Minister at King Avenue. The new appointment brought challenges both to Grayson Atha and to the congregation. Recognizing, as a group, that homosexuals within our congregation raised an issue, The Homosexuality Study Committee was created. The Homosexuality Study Committee was charged with presenting a policy recommendation for the church regarding our official position on homosexuality.

At this time, the church was made up of many more theologically-conservative members and students, as well as a group of more liberal-leaning persons. Then there was a group of gay people who, although very closeted, were thinking of the possibility of a church that would openly embrace the gay population of the neighborhood.

It was within this setting that the need for the Committee became evident. The Committee was chaired by Bob Heber, a retired personnel manager who had been a long time member of King Avenue. It was Mr. Heber who chaired the Staff Parish Relations Committee when I came to King Avenue. The Committee met twice each month for seven months.

When all was said and done, the Committee recommended that King Avenue welcome all people and that words such as homosexual, gay, lesbian, and other related words could be spoken in context at King Avenue.

My Time at King Avenue is Extended
After the Report of The Committee and its adoption by the Administrative Council, the Bishop informed the church she intended to continue to appoint me as the Senior Pastor. The announcement was made on a Sunday morning and was greeted with an ovation.

If you attend King Avenue today, you will find a church that welcomes all, has a large number of children and young families, as well as persons of all ages.

The membership has grown from 400 to over 800, and the worship attendance has risen from 250 to presently 550.

If you should worship at King Avenue Church today, you will find a warm, vibrant, welcoming congregation where no one is afraid of who they are.

After twelve years as the senior pastor of King Avenue, I reached the age of 70, the age at which *The United Methodist Book of Discipline* requires pastors to retire.

Did I go happy and willingly? I wouldn't say that. Did I revert back to the "neighbor and fence" scenario just a little by not drawing a line in the sand regarding ageism and discrimination? Perhaps. Did I find it a little ironic that I was "asked" to leave this church a second time, not because of my ministry, or leadership style, but because of a number by which my usefulness was being judged? Sure.

Did my children "motion" me to rise up against this type of age discrimination that most of society has already rejected, the type of mandate that flies in the face of the older adults who make up the largest portions of many of our congregations? Indeed they did. In fact they motioned me in the light of day, and their motions reverberated with me deep into some of my nights.

But the riches I left King Avenue with were enough to make my heart overflow. They were enough to give me strength for the next opportunity God has for me, enough to keep my heart, my mind, and my door open for whatever the future holds. I guess, with all that in mind, I could allow this particular "property line" of my ministry to be defined by *The United Methodist Book of Discipline* and the present Bishop.

This will be a great moment of challenge and opportunity in the life of King Avenue UMC, for the congregation will soon discover that the changes made have put them in charge of their destiny.

With this in mind, and following the Christ who teaches us that every person is of great worth, and a church full of people who have experienced the presence of the Holy Spirit in their midst, they are ready to walk into the future knowing nothing can separate them from the Love of God in Christ Jesus.

As for me, I will look back with gratitude for having served, for the final twelve years of active ministry, a church willing to risk and struggle so all may know the love of God.

Peace,

Grayson

Postscript

When I retired, at age 70, I began to adjust to a new life. It did not go well. I missed the interaction with people, the preparation of sermons, being on the edge of church conflict (yes, it's true I kind of liked the conflict). I realized I still wanted to minister to people as they encountered milestones that helped shape their lives, and their faith.

In the United Methodist Church there is a provision for a person to serve in a retired relationship, so I decided to go for it! Early on, I completed a one-month appointment at Good Shepherd UMC, a church on the north side of Columbus which was in transition at the time. Then I was appointed to William Street UMC across from the Ohio Wesleyan University campus. Following that, I spent three years at Summit UMC on the campus of The Ohio State University. In 2012, I was appointed to Gates Fourth UMC, located just south of German Village in Columbus.

These have all been different but wonderful experiences. I suppose one day I will fade away. But the people of these churches have provided energy and meaning for my life. And that meaning will go with me as I fade. It will always be a part of me.

Postscript from a Friend

As a young professional working and living in Cincinnati, Ohio in the 1990's, I often had occasion to drive between the prestigious neighborhoods of Mount Adams and Hyde Park travelling by way of Madison Avenue. In leaving either of these two well-heeled, upscale neighborhoods for the other, I would cross through East Walnut Hills, a part of town that struck me because of the dramatic change in landscape. Historic houses lining the street went from freshly painted to barely painted. Storefronts and restaurants that were richly adorned and seating trendy mostly white patrons became skeletal buildings hailed by wooden windows, and hand painted signs. Dusting the streets in East Walnut Hills were the town's inhabitants, African Americans, greeting each other as they walked from here to there, or to nowhere in particular. Inside this stark contrast of Cincinnati's neighboring towns was yet another one. There as I travelled through downtown East Walnut Hills was a wispy haired white man, standing alone or talking joyfully with others of the town's residents, near or on the steps of an old stone church off Madison Ave. I always noticed this man because he was out of place.

Over a decade later, I was introduced to the Reverend Grayson Atha. A friend suggested I might like to attend King Avenue Church, and I recall my surprise on my first Sunday, when I heard Reverend Atha say the words "gay and lesbian", not followed by the usual condemnations (actually he said "gay and lesbian luncheon" and I was shocked to know that not only were we not condemned in this church - we were apparently fed lunch). As a closeted gay Christian, Grayson was the first Minister to have contact with the real me, not the one I had taken to church for all those years of Sundays and ushered out the back before anyone could ask my name. As a member of Grayson's church, I was personally and deeply affected by his love, his example, and his commitment to opening the doors of the church to gay, lesbian, and transgendered members. Soon, Grayson invited me to work closely with him in leading a ministry connecting our church in direct and meaningful service to poor and homeless persons living in our community. This single experience changed me more than all my years sitting in pews ever had. This is how he touches lives. He gets involved and gets us involved. Over the past 15 years since meeting Grayson, I have only experienced his tirelessness in loving others, leading social change, and developing better understandings between people who are fundamentally different.

At some point, I learned through Grayson's daughter Angelyn, that he had once been the pastor of an all black church in East Walnut Hills in Cincinnati. I quickly realized that the wispy haired white man I had seen all those years ago on Madison Avenue was actually Grayson. Turns out now after knowing him, that in opposition to what I thought at the time, he wasn't out of place there at all. He was very much in place.

Chris Prespare
Charleston, Illinois

Made in the USA
Monee, IL
05 October 2023

44004502R00101